What people are saying about ...

Thirsting

"Deep souls in an era of distraction are a vanishing species. Even rarer are those few deep souls who can lovingly invite us away from our diversions into life with God. My friend Strahan is one of our modern-day desert fathers. A quiet, wise voice in a world of noise. If you want to hear God, follow this teacher, read this book, say yes to this path—the true path of prayer."

John Mark Comer, *New York Times* bestselling
author and founder of Practicing the Way

"In poetic prose, Strahan Coleman strings together a compelling picture of prayer that is equally melodic and earthy—widening the eyes in wonder, enflaming the heart with desire, and also somehow staying grounded enough to embody in practice. *Thirsting* reads like a book that's been lived deeply prior to being written, and that sort of book, while sadly a rarity, carries the most potent message."

Tyler Staton, lead pastor of Bridgetown Church

"Saint Augustine famously said, 'Lord, put salt on our lips that we would thirst for you.' This book will thoroughly salt your lips! Many times, as I read this book, I would have to put it down and let the love of God wash over me. It taps into the deepest longings of our soul and paints such an eloquent picture of why those longings are there and the God who is waiting to be found at the end of them. It helped me understand in a profound way that God is not only the giver of these longings but is their fulfilment. Strahan is a modern-day mystic, inviting the church to sink deeper into the mystery of love found in a triune God and to join him as a fellow mystic, deepening our experience and understanding of that love. This book stirred me, called me home, and acted as a portal into God's presence. All who are thirsty, come and read!"

Sam Harvey, BMin, national coordinator
of 24–7 Prayer New Zealand and
pastor of Bay Vineyard Church

"Strahan has beautifully and deeply invited us to come to the fountain of life and bathe our thirsty souls in Jesus. I can't think of a more important message for a thirsty generation."

Al Gordon, SAINT

"Strahan Coleman reminds us that every human has a fundamental posture toward the transcendent, a draw toward the Divine. You can feel that draw in his work, even in the pages of this book."

John Mark McMillan, songwriter
and recording artist

"As a masterful narrator of the raw parts of our hearts, Strahan invites us to be honest with our longings and introduces us, or reintroduces us, to our Friend who loves to meet us in those honest and thirsty places. My parched spirit continues to be encouraged by Coleman's honest and generous work."

Zach Meerkreebs, pastor in residence at Asbury University and author of *Lower: Igniting Spiritual Awakening through Radical Humility*

"I want to give this book to everyone I know! As someone who spent years striving by force of will to make deeper connection with God, in this book, my friend, Strahan, describes exactly my own eventual realization: God is not a stern taskmaster but a relentless pursuer who thirsts to marry each one of us. 'Having it together doesn't qualify us for Christ, only desperation, only need, only thirst.' 'The gospel isn't a story so much of our pursuit of God, but of God's pursuit of us. Of His thirst for us.' In this wonderful book, Strahan shows us how knowing and living out of this truth can make all the difference."

Sr. Dorcee Clarey

"Strahan has a way of writing on spiritual matters that makes the reader feel like they're spending time with a close friend. And it just so happens that he is my friend, and what you read in this book is an authentic expression of what one experiences being around him."

Jason Upton, songwriter and worship leader

Thirsting

Thirsting

quenching

our

soul's

deepest

desire

STRAHAN COLEMAN

DAVID C COOK®

transforming lives together

THIRSTING
Published by David C Cook
4050 Lee Vance Drive
Colorado Springs, CO 80918 U.S.A.

Integrity Music Limited, a Division of David C Cook
Brighton, East Sussex BN1 2RE, England

DAVID C COOK® and related marks are registered trademarks of David C Cook.

The website addresses recommended throughout this book are offered as a
resource to you. These websites are not intended in any way to be or imply an
endorsement on the part of David C Cook, nor do we vouch for their content.

Details in some stories have been changed to protect
the identities of the persons involved.

Bible credits appear at the end of the book.

Library of Congress Control Number 2024940878
ISBN 978-0-8307-8520-9
eISBN 978-0-8307-8521-6

The Team: Michael Covington, Stephanie Bennett, Caroline
Cilento, James Hershberger, Susan Murdock
Cover Design: Faceout Studios, Spencer Fuller

Printed in the United States of America
First Edition 2024

1 2 3 4 5 6 7 8 9 10

062824

For Bruce Gilberd

Contents

"God thirsts that we would thirst for Him."

Saint Augustine

Author's Note

Let me begin with a caution: if I've written this book right, it will be a liberating but dangerous invitation. Nothing has marked my life greater than my wholehearted pursuit of God, and nothing has wounded me more deeply. Because God, in His extravagant love, will refuse anything within us that would hinder us from our full engulfing in His astronomical want of us. Love, by nature, refuses to be separated in any way from its object.

God wants our all.

That sounds romantic until He comes for the things in us we don't want to give away. Not so much material things as our insecurities, our fears, our self-protection. Because often what's treasure to the world is fodder to God, and what we think of as off limits in our hearts is exactly where Christ will venture to free us even more.

Love is liberation, but we're prone to loving our chains.

And this *is* a love story.

Always in this world, great treasures cost us the most. Be they gold, jewels, Olympic achievements, or finding and keeping the love of our lives. If an athlete has to give up everything else to obtain gold, and if in marriage we say no to every other person on earth that we may have our *yes* with the one, then how much more will receiving the whole of Love cost us.

But the good news is, giving up and giving over to this Love is far more like winning the lottery than a prison sentence. Because whatever we give up, whatever we go through, pales in comparison to the inconceivable love and freedom we're returned in the presence of the Beloved.

There is no treasure on earth like the living of God in the depth of our souls, and once we get a taste for it, this Love that desires us, we discover in us a thirst to give ourselves wholly over to it. The cost evaporates.

We're free to become more free.

This is the greatest story known. Once we hear it, and let it in, we can never be the same again. It calls to each of us, to our dormant, unlit places, that with its penetrating light it may finally wake us up.

I imagine you're reading this book because, like me, you either thirst for God or thirst to thirst for Him. More importantly, you're here because the Holy Spirit has drawn you. Because the very existence of your thirst, your desperation, is the sign that God is already beginning to meet it.

Even if you're numb, barren, or lost, underneath what may feel like the wilderness of you is the groaning of the Spirit crying out for more of His Father on your behalf.[1] So if you're afraid God may not hear your cries for divine hydration, you can know with certainty He will hear His own.

What follows is an invitation to give your *yes* in ever-deepening relent to the power of God's love filling and resting in your being. It's to the satisfaction of this very thirst of your existence. More importantly, it's to the realisation of how little our thirst truly is in comparison to that of Love's.

This is about letting *the* Thirst in, opening our very soul to Him, and learning to receive this meeting of thirsts as the divine calling we were all made for.

What follows is a road map for a life of holy intimacy. A life of belovedness. An awakening of the fire of love within us that we might thirst with greater fervour for the Lover of our souls.

Reader, if you're not ready for love, continue at your own risk.

Preface

My son and I were having a late night conversation recently when, out of the blue, he asked, "Dad, how can I become a saint?" A few weeks earlier I'd been sharing stories about great Christian lives with him, stories that are hard to believe yet inspiringly true of people fully given over to God's love in this life. He'd obviously been stewing on it. He had a growing interest it seemed in joining what Paul called the "great cloud of witnesses."[2]

But the question stumped me. There were a dozen ways to answer it. It would've been easy to talk about the miraculous things saints of the past had done, their teaching, poetry, miracles, or the hospitals and schools they founded. But that wouldn't get to the heart of it. What they did was incredible, but the whole idea of a saint is precisely that their lives were exceptional and in many ways unattainable. Like a top sportsman or a great inventor, they are examples of profound grace that inspire us all toward a better life.

Just trying to do great things could send my son off on a life of self-dependence and striving, thinking that significance comes from quantity and notoriety. Wanting to be a saint bad enough and striving in self-effort to achieve it definitely won't make you one.

But I didn't want to tell him that it's all emotional and interior either. Saints are saints not only because they were people of prayer, but because they engaged with the world and gave us a vision for making it better. Who they were was the gift, what they did was their legacy.

Still not quite sure how to define a saint, and what it looks like to be one, I paused and, after a little silence, replied, "Let me tell you a story."

I told him about the most formative experiences of my life. Times of intense seeking when I was a young man, calling out to God to meet me. I told him how I would ache for nothing else. How, when I realised just how little I loved and just how little of God I had, I desired desperately for more. I told him that when my friends went out on weekends, I stayed home, crying on my knees on the floor, telling God that if I couldn't have Him, life would be unbearable. I had to have Him, to be consumed by Him.

As I shared all this with my son, my own heart was moved. Tears welled up as I remembered it, how close God became to me and how ever since He has been answering that same prayer over and over, day by day.

"I don't know how to become a saint, son," I said, "but I know this. It begins *there*."

Tears were filling his eyes as well. He was still, sitting quietly, feeling the weight of the moment.

I've spent years talking with my sons about the Love of my life, spanning theology, science, morality, and personal experience. But it's often felt intellectual, like it wasn't getting to the heart. I wondered how to help it land just how close God is for me, how crucial, how defining.

Now, all of that was transcended. In this moment, my son saw his dad vulnerable, incapable, desperate. He saw, maybe for the first time, just how much I *need* God, how much I want Him, and it moved him.

We sat together there for a while, feeling it, stewing in the wonder of the presence that filled our hearts. It's possible that very conversation will burn in his memory for years to come. I hope it does. I hope it lives in him as a monument for what this faith is all about, and what it means to be a saint.

To me, it felt like he was hearing the gospel for the first time.

That night, I believe, he encountered his *thirst*.

"If Anyone Thirsts"

Sweetest Love,
amidst the cries and toils
of my dehydration,
it is, has always been
and will be forever,
You that I thirst for.

Chapter 1

To Be a Saint

*"My love for You has gone
far deeper than I can feel.
It has become a deep fire.
It has become Your fire."*

Prayer Vol. 04

Søren Kierkegaard said that to be a saint, to have purity of heart, "is to will one thing," to *want* one thing, we could say.[3] But how do we do that? How do we learn to long, and to long ever deeper for, this Beloved who created and seeks our hearts?

The greatest commandment is to love God with all of ourselves, but have you ever wondered how we can simply love more than we do? Is it an invitation to will our way into affection and devotion to God? Because if it is, it sounds more like being set up for failure than freedom.

Longing, and longing for God, has been the defining force of my life since those nights on my knees in my early twenties. I've wanted, with every fibre, to love and experience God's love, and just as often, I've ached at the emptiness of that love within me, and the insignificance of my spiritual flame.

It's been said that "desire is the straw that stirs the drink" of our lives.[4] That at the very bottom of it all, at the very heart of the gospel, is the reorientation of our deepest yearnings, a resurrection of divine affection, an encounter of love. In this view the kingdom of heaven, at its core, isn't ultimately about eternal security, ethics, moralism, or justice, but desire. Desire is the blood rushing through the veins of all Christian spirituality.

It's also the very heart of prayer. It could be said that all of the biblical story is simply one big love letter from God to humanity, to you personally, to me, saying "I want you"—not only love but *want*. That beneath the low hum of human consciousness, hidden amidst molecules and atoms, in the sound of the wind touching trees, the gentle lapping of the shore's waters, and in the outstretched arms of a Nazarene carpenter, one aching question has defined all existence since "Let there be": "Will you love Me back?"

The whole gospel is simply an invitation to respond "Yes" with all our being.

We are, you are, being pursued.

In movements and language unfamiliar to your life-worn senses, Divine Love wants you, is after you in your deepest places. This pursuit is so much more than an existential exchange, it's a deep calling to deep longing for the mingling of your being with He who created you. It's what you were made for.

If there were a manual for your soul, it would show that all its functions, fine tunings, and settings are calibrated for this. This world, this life, may have worn the engine or rusted the joints, but none of that can change the intention. You were made for love, love is the fuel that heals you.

And love *thirsts*.

This very pursuit magnetises all of us. At the bottom of our being is a throbbing, an aching that pines for its *Other* day and night, in endless longing. That part of us knows. Knows that everything else unsatisfies, knows there's something non-external that wants to find its way in. Knows that a soul-longing can't be fulfilled by anything this world has to offer, despite the world's best efforts to convince us so.

We may not know how to articulate it, maybe we're not even conscious of it yet, but our deeper self thirsts. It's driving our entire life. It's not alone either, because our longing is an echo of a love spoken deep into the cavern of us, aching to return to its Source.

We thirst because we're thirsted *for*.

Deep calling to deep.

Love is a tale of two longings.

These two realities, Love's pursuit of us and our deep calling back, are the tension that lives beneath the cosmos, driving everything that exists. Our spiritual journey toward union with God erupts, grows, and is defined by our awakening to this loving tension. It lies at the centre of our story, of God's people, of you and me as individuals.

We thirst, and for more than just a brief brush with Love. For more than even a friendship with it. We thirst for permanent saturation. To be *married* to Eternity.

This pilgrimage involves the soul. It involves our learning to open up the very foundation of us, where we feel most uncertain and vulnerable, where we long so deeply that we're afraid to expose it to any *other* for fear of rejection. There, if we allow it, in the very place of our greatest vulnerability, in the place of our *thirst*, Desire Himself longs gently to arrive to commune with us.

That's what it means to wed Love, to be "filled with the Spirit," to call God "Beloved." A Spirit-to-soul intermingling, a living from this deepest well.

But that's no easy feat. Unloving things happen to and around us in life and we find ourselves building internal walls to insulate our insecurities. Because of the ensuing vulnerability we feel when it comes to our deepest, loving self, we could be forgiven for considering it better to be called to some far-off mission field than brave exposing our greatest hopes and longings to God.

Giving our outer life to God, for many of us, is far less threatening than opening up our inner one. We may be able to imagine His saving us, His using and even loving us, but *wanting* us? *Pursuing* us? Pursuing *me* there? That's something else entirely.

And yet, that's precisely the truth. God wants you, pursues you, and wants to live inside you not to make you some kind of "host" for

His mission on earth, but to commune in the very depths of your soul where you are your most naked, true, and alive.

Thirst isn't so much about passion, although it's a vital part of it. Passion is the intense good feelings we get when we're doing something or being with someone we love. Passion is important and God-given, but it's not always the deepest place to live from. Passion ebbs and flows with sickness, circumstance, and seasons. Feelings change, storms come, challenges arrive, and sometimes our feelings deceive us.

If we equate love for God with passion, we'll be tossed by the waves of it for all our days. Passion is best served by something deeper, more permanent and sure. Something we all have, even if at times it lives deeper than our ability to access it. That is, desire.

Desire dwells in the very core of who we are. It's non-negotiable. It's what drives us. It's our compulsion toward life, love, ambition, or otherwise. Desire is the aquifer that feeds the well of passion. It's underneath. It's a powerful living force. When we touch our desire, we touch the very engine of our souls, that which is steady through any season, a current so deep it's untouched by the surface swell of the storms that come to us in this life. We touch our thirst.

COME AND DRINK

In John's gospel we find Jesus standing in the marketplace, crying, "If anyone thirsts ... come to me and drink."[5] It was the last day of a great feast, the verse also tells us, and Jesus chose this moment to stand in the middle of the jubilant crowds and declare that *He* was the object of humanity's desire. Right there, when the people had everything they needed to fill their stomachs within reach, at the peak of celebration, joy, and community, Jesus pointed to Himself as if to say, "It's Me, I'm the one, all this is just the entrée."

Today, in this "easy access, goods saturated, whatever we want at our fingertips" world, He's doing the same. He's calling us heavenward, to feast on something richer and more satisfying than anything in this world.

God longs for us to drink Him.

Beneath our pain, our cautious hopes and desperate longings, the Spirit gently speaks to us, lovingly and persistently asking, "Beloved, will you love Me back? Will you 'will this one thing'?"

Jesus, when He says, "If anyone thirsts" is, of course, being ironic. We are *all* people who thirst. You and I are far more than mere machines in need of maintenance, our ache is existential, spiritual, eternal. We long for love, meaning, legacy, significance. There's not a human on earth who doesn't feel it though plenty of us refuse to face it for fear of what we'll find.

And so we begin here, with ourselves and our learning to feel, touch, and name our thirst. We live amidst powers and principalities that fear such an awakening, that want nothing more for us than to stay blind to what we truly want so they can keep marketing us the latest products and their lesser visions of life. Desire begins with awakening, then quickly becomes an act of resistance.

This resistance requires a vision. One found first in who God is as trinity, and the yearning discovered in His story of pursuing humanity since "Let there be." In God's yearning we discover the beauty, goodness, and vitality of divine desire and what it can do for us in bringing us Home. We find our map too, for going deeper into prayer. We discover God's desire to be one with us.

Secondly, Jesus was making a statement about the *end* of all that longing. Its nature is personal, it is God's very self. In a world where we could turn anywhere else, Jesus tells us "come to me" if we really want to drink. He makes Himself available to us, breaking through the religious barrier of separation, our fears, anxieties, and shame. There are no moral or religious prerequisites here. Having it together doesn't qualify us for Christ, only desperation, only need, only thirst.

The issue is universal, the solution personal. There is nowhere else on earth to go. God alone can quench us.

But we have to learn what that means, this "coming" to Him. It's an all of ourselves experience that involves the soul, the mind, and what we do with our bodies. Thirsting isn't only some kind of detached, ethereal experience, it's a deeply human one rooted in our thoughts and actions. We need to discern His movements, to learn to receive His Spirit in our *deepest self.*

Finally, Jesus invites us to experience Him, to "drink." This is a promise of internality, a promise to fill us with His presence, to quench the depths of us with love. He could have said He would simply wash or anoint us with His waters, but He didn't. He told us to drink, promising that His very life and love would find its way down into the deepest and darkest places of our being, filling us with Life.

This is an invitation to a kind of prayer many of us aren't used to. It's here we learn to be a *soul*, to dwell in deeper places, and to brave opening ourselves up to Love in ways we may have never done before. It's here, in our growing into the intermingling life promised by Jesus, that we discover prayer as nakedness, as liberating acceptance, as relent.

All our work in naming thirst, discovering its Origin, awakening to the beauty of desire and our bringing our lives into its shape, is about arriving here in the last quarter of the book. It's about a new liberation.

Know your thirst, step over fear and shame, receive God's love, drink Him deeply.

That's the gospel.

That's also, to me, what it means to be a saint.

Over these recent years of my own faith life, reckoning with the ache within me has found itself centre stage. Moving to a small town in the Covid years and slowly sinking into a quieter, slower rhythm of life helped bring a whole lot of unconscious longing to the surface of me again. It's forced me to face some old pains and fears around health, vocation, and self that I thought I'd put to rest in previous seasons.

But more than all of that, it's been a time of discovering whole new dimensions of love. Not my ability to love. The opposite, in fact. What I've really come to grasp is my inability to love, and God's profound and passionate love in the face of it. A revelation that only made me long and thirst even more. And so, amidst quiet winters and the sparseness of small-town life, I've spent my time facing the pain of my longings and owning the gap that exists between heaven and my heart—what I hope for and want in God and life, and what is my reality.

I've opened up myself to God where it's liberating and where it's terrifying and I've observed and experienced God's passion for my deeper places. For communing with me there. I've learned to unravel myself, to feel weaker, to experience love there in my vulnerability and to slowly, become comfortable living that way.

Everything that follows is what I've come to learn through it all. It's about deeper drinking. A saying yes to Jesus' invitation to find soul-level hydration in the waters of Him.

That's where we're going from here. Beginning first with our naming and articulating this force, this gift within us we call desire.

> *Father, awaken us now to love,*
> *to that very question that holds*
> *us in existence—Your heavenly ache;*
> *that we may discover not only You,*
> *but ourselves, in the liberation*
> *of hearing You say, "beloved."*

Chapter 2

On Thirst

"If longing in every form is prayer,
then my soul is ceaseless towards You."

Prayer Vol. 02

We are searching, all of us, for so many things. For love, for meaning, for success. Sometimes that searching is more of a running from something, be it trauma, disappointment, or fear, but most of the time it's simply an attempt to fill our spiritual stomachs to relieve the existential hunger we feel but can't touch and name.

We all are magnets, born unable to stop ourselves driving towards satiating this existential thirst. That's not to say that we always know how to articulate that experience. Many can't even acknowledge it at times. But it exists as the turbine that propels the world into its booms and busts nonetheless.

To be human is to thirst. To thirst to make whole what feels so *un*whole within us. Our economy depends on it. Smart individuals have made their wealth by pulling the strings of that desire to their own ends. If we all stopped trying to fill that thirst with food, clothing, sex, technology, money, travel, or information, even if we just drastically moderated it, our economies would experience immediate trauma.

It is inseparable from human existence. In fact, the Hebrew word for "soul" in the Old Testament, *nephesh*, can mean "thirst." To be human is to be a living thirst container. We can deny that we feel it, but it will only drive us harder. If we're not careful, it will enslave us. We can try to rationalise or domesticate it through consumerism or some other means, but on our weakest days, when our defences are down, it will spring up like a tiger from the bushes and consume us.

Where and how we direct this energy has been the subject of philosophers and pundits alike for millennia, because it often feels out of our control, unbridled. Aristotle, the famous Greek philosopher from the fourth century BC, is attributed as saying, "I count him braver who overcomes his desires than him who conquers his enemies; for the hardest victory is over self," and Paul the apostle famously reflected, "What I want to do I do not do, but what I hate I do."[6] Anyone who has ever tried to do the opposite of what their body drives them towards will sympathise.

And yet despite the ability of this fundamental thirst to taunt and rule us, the Scriptures teach us that it is *good*, not a mistake or aberration. God declared early in our story that "it is not good for man to be alone,"[7] showing us that even totally naked and open before God and creation (and before our fall), humanity had a thirst for more than just self-sufficiency. We cannot find our whole-ness within ourselves, we are made with an *other*-thirst. As a single piece in the divine puzzle of intimacy. The longing for goodness, for beauty and truth, is embedded in our ancient story.

Later the psalmists, our great teachers of prayer, refused to squash nor squander their thirst, directing it instead toward their Maker, crying, "My soul thirsts for God, for the living God," and again, "My soul thirsts for you; my flesh faints for you, as in a dry and weary land where there is no water."[8]

In both verses the psalmists used the Hebrew word *nephesh* for "soul," which literally means "throat." For them, there was no delin-eation between spiritual and physical thirst. Their bodies' longings weren't disconnected from the aches of the heart, they harmonised with each other in a love song to their Maker. The thirst of our bodies, of our living, is a sign of something inward. We were made entirely to be filled by Another.

This is vital, because in our post-enlightened world we're prone to compartmentalising ourselves into mind, body, and spirit. But human beings were made with each in harmonious unity. That means that our philosophical longings are an expression of our thirst for God, as is our daily need for food and water, our emotional ache for acceptance and intimacy, and our souls' magnetism to be *in* that which we love. With every fibre of our being, we thirst by design.

Jesus Himself would come to bless our thirst when, in describ-ing the shape of His coming kingdom on earth, He proclaimed, "Blessed are those who hunger and thirst for righteousness, for they will be filled."[9] Showing that it's precisely our *deficit*, according to

Jesus, that beckons the miracle. Our need that invites the provision of His very self.

It's significant then that when Jesus does say "If anyone thirsts, let him come to *me* and drink," He does it standing in the middle of a festival precisely when we're filling our minds, hearts, and stomachs with the goodness of this world. Here, when everything seems to be at our fingertips, Jesus reminds us of the End of all that pleasure, Himself. All those things are good gifts, but they don't satisfy. Jesus knows it. Deep down I believe we all do.

If we don't experience, feel, and articulate our thirst, we'll never know the Love that seeks to satisfy it. Thirst, as it turns out, is the currency of the kingdom of heaven, one that Jesus tells us fuels the economy of His presence.

God makes thirst holy.

RECKONING WITH DIS-EASE

It's not always easy, however, to understand what coming to drink God actually feels like or even how to go about opening up to God in the first place. Because the truth is, just knowing that we thirst can't always help us, precisely because it's so ravenous and violent that it overcomes our sensibilities and leads us at its whims.

Anyone who has struggled with any level of addiction (which I believe is all of us to some extent) will tell you that knowing something is unhealthy for us, or even wanting to give it up, often holds little power against the torrent of bodily drive that sends us running toward it in our weakest moments.

If thirst is so good, then why can it be such a tyrant? Why is it so hard to reckon with? In trying to manage it, we discover that our thirst is a force that drives us in both the good and the bad. The known and the unknown. If a soul had gravity, this would be it, for better or for worse.

Ronald Rolheiser describes this as our *dis-ease*, a little fire we're born with that is more human disposition than occasional visit:

> We are not easeful human beings who occasion-
> ally get restless, serene persons who once in a while
> are obsessed by desire. The reverse is true. We are
> driven persons, forever obsessed, congenitally dis-
> eased, living lives, as Thoreau once suggested, of
> quiet desperation, only occasionally experiencing
> peace. Desire is the straw that stirs the drink.[10]

Again, that doesn't mean that desire is wrong. Our dis-ease is only a *disease* if we allow it to rule over us. But it is to say that's a reality for all of us. Opting in is not a thing, it will either unseat or liberate us. There's no middle ground.

Saint Augustine said, "He who loses himself in his passion is less lost than he who loses his passion."[11] He would say that our thirst makes us alive, makes us lovers, drives us toward our Good End. That it's a sign of life. To lose it, we could then argue, is more dangerous than to misspend it. If you've ever lost your taste for life, or known someone who has, you might agree.

And yet we don't often associate this raw desire within us as our divine homing beacon. Thirst, in all its forms, is often presented (or experienced) as a threat by many in the church. It's something we've come to fear, or at least have no place to home in our faith. To many of us, Augustine's statement sounds like near heresy. Spiritual maturity seems to become about becoming more detached, cool, immovable, and serious.

One of the great fallacies of some church teaching has been to deny or suppress the beauty of our thirst rather than celebrate it as part of our essential spiritual life. In the vacuum of having no positive theology for desire, we make it our enemy, trying to pretend it away.

It's a promise unkeepable, though, because if our thirst *is* God-given as we'll soon see, trying to do away with it will only harm us. Eventually, it will squeeze out the sides of us when we're not paying attention. The fallout of which we've seen all too often in recent years.

In our own lives this can look like periods of intense consecration toward God followed by seasonal outbursts of self-destructive behaviour. A see-saw that is a sure sign that we don't yet have a redeemed love of longing.

Suppressing our thirst makes us unhealthier, not holier.

Our dis-ease carries with it a demand for reckoning. Not only when it's denied but when it's idolised, too. Allowing our desire to determine what is good and who God is has caused just as much confusion and harm. As we'll explore, discerning among our thirsts is crucial if we're to walk the Way the whole journey home.

Giving in to whatever thirsts we feel is no liberation. In the ancient world, thirst was seen as something to be mastered. Since God's warning to Cain that "if you do not do what is right, sin is crouching at your door; it desires to have you, but you must rule over it,"[12] we have sought to curb our distorted thirsts toward goodness and ancient religions, and philosophies sought to domesticate them through ritual, rite, and discipline. First by philosophising about what goodness and truth really are before exploring forms of asceticism that hope to turn the mind, body, and soul toward that end. The Old Testament is a long story of humanity's failure to do so with all the willpower it could muster.

Today, however, giving in to our thirsts is widely celebrated. In fact, the Western hero of the moment is often the person who throws off all exterior pressures—family, cultural boundaries, tradition, and social restrictions—to be and do whatever they want. Few places reveal this more than the astoundingly popular kids movie *Frozen*, where the protagonist Elsa sings her song of liberation: "It's time to see what I can do / To test the limits and break through / No right, no wrong, no rules for me / I'm free."[13]

Few people today would bat an eyelid at that hyper-individual view. Choosing or being whatever we want has simply become what freedom *is* to us. Being driven from the inside. No restrictions. For the ancient mind, giving in to the whims of our thirst was madness, today it's heroic. A brief glance at Western society as a whole is enough to see it's not doing us the good we'd hoped.

This culture of giving in is no accident either. It is, in fact, a twentieth-century design. In *The Patterning Instinct: A Cultural History of Humanity's Search for Meaning*, Jeremy Lent summarises the mentality of the movement toward a thirst-based economy:

> We must shift America from a needs to a desires culture.... People must be trained to desire, to want new things, even before the old have been entirely consumed. We must shape a new mentality. Man's desires must overshadow his needs.[14]

We don't live in neutral territory when it comes to the desires of our hearts, we are part of a masterful system that longs to manipulate and use our thirst to its own ends. Human thirst is so fundamental, it's become a commodity. If we're going to rediscover our fire for God, we need to recognize this war taking place for it every day, and do something about it.

This battle over our thirst is being waged against us by the wealthiest and most powerful organisations in the world and, almost more terrifyingly, algorithms that instinctively play on our weakness and insecurities. Our God-given thirst has been colonised, monetised, and manipulated to no end. We've been trained to spend it anywhere but where it matters most.

What matters in this consumer-oriented world we live in is not curbing our thirst towards what is needed, good, and right, but living in perpetual thirst so as to grow our economy and satisfy our whims.

Each day we wake up, every advertisement and message we see seeks to convince us this or that item will finally make us happy, beautiful, or satisfied. Think of the way advertising has changed. Fewer than a hundred years ago an advertisement for a good would consist of a picture and paragraphs of text describing the item and its usefulness. Today, we're more likely to see a doctored and unrealistically perfect person beside the item being advertised, expressing innuendo hardly, or not at all, related to the product itself.

It's no longer the good itself and its relevance to us that matter, only that we're made to think it will satisfy our wants. No matter how ridiculous the connection being made. Billboards now litter our streets crying, "Come to me all who thirst, and I will give you my product!"

Manufactured desire sells the world now, not reality.

One could argue that what began as a drive to grow the economy has become the DNA of Western culture and, even worse, internalised itself as a spirituality. We've come to believe that getting all the time will satisfy us, that just a little more and we'll be content. Slowly, we've made not God the end of our longing, but the things He made us. Eating them up with increasing voracity only to feed a painful discontent in our prayer lives.

The cultural idealist today follows their heart's greatest thirst, be it for another, ideally more perfect, husband or wife to satisfy the whims of the body's wants, to hoard money toward unthinkable greed, or to just act in whatever way feels personally right rather than have an external religious, moral, or philosophical system dictate it to them. A "my truth" movement.

Marketers keep selling us the idea we'll get there and be satisfied, because the illusion keeps us spending. Interesting how the rise of access to all the things we want coincides with the rise of pharmaceutical drugs to medicate the disappointment when we do actually get them.

If the fruit of the Spirit is self-control, the fruit of the age is self-gratification.

Despite the world's catch cry to come and drink it, medication for anxiety and depression is so widely used it's traceable in drinking water the world over.[15] We live in perpetual dissatisfaction. The more boundaries we break, the more we discover that there's no contentment over the hill. Drinking the world this way is like trying to hydrate on alcohol. The more we drink, the thirstier we become until we're ill from the chase. We are lost to our thirsts and slowly coming to realise that not reckoning with it will be the end of our joy.

To make matters worse, in contrast to this apparent liberation the world offers us, religion is painted as oppressive, restrictive, and anti-human. Like a grumpy neighbour who hates the sound of children laughing and playing in the streets. I often wonder if subconsciously many Christians feel the same way, that Jesus' teaching runs counter to and not in harmony with the satisfaction of our longings.

How often do you hear people talking of the *goodness* of Jesus' teachings and the liberation obeying them brings? More often, they're painted as repressive and domineering. Things we do to please God, not to be more alive. As we'll see later, in the "Fidelity" chapter, nothing could be further from the truth. Jesus' teachings are the language of love, themselves the way in which we drink deeper of God's loving presence.

ENTER NUMBNESS

There's another tragic by-product to all this unchained thirsting and that's the numbness that comes from the realisation that what the world is offering is an unkeepable promise. Because even when we get what we *think* we want, we're still often left feeling empty. Our satisfaction is fleeting, here and gone in a moment. Gradually, the buzz of our getting stops giving us the hit it used to and we lose the motivation to keep trying.

In her book *Dopamine Nation*, Dr. Anna Lembke explains that the brain has a pleasure-pain system, constantly balancing the two like a see-saw to ensure we don't go off the deep end of one or the other. As it turns out, if we overstimulate on pleasure through dopamine, the brain will then overcorrect with pain generating to balance it.

Lembke goes on to say, "The paradox is that hedonism, the pursuit of pleasure for its own sake, leads to *anhedonia*, which is an inability to enjoy pleasure of any kind."[16] The secular myth of the self-life leading to satisfaction is as much a scientific misnomer, according to Lembke, as a spiritual one. In other words, just seeking to gratify our thirsts on whatever temporal highs are around us only leads to greater pain. Soon enough we can find ourselves exactly where Augustine warns us we don't want to be: passionless.

It turns out that the body needs both pleasure *and* pain to be healthy, but we don't hear that message from the marketplace corners of our world. In light of this, Jesus' invitation to "take up [your] cross and follow me"[17] takes on a whole new wisdom. A wisdom we'll explore in part 3 of this book when we discover what it means to pray our pain.

In practice, this oversaturation of pleasure has led to a pervasive numbness in our generation. One that, without intention, has crept in and set like concrete in many of our spiritual lives. For some of us, having uncontrollable thirst is less of a problem than feeling no desire at all. We come to live a tasteless life, a tasteless faith. For us, there is no sense of pleasure in life at all, let alone in God. We are watchers of the world only, wondering how a dull heart comes awake again after the disappointments of getting what we thought we wanted without any real life from it. How to fan a tiny flame into a wildfire of thirst for God.

I know all too well the feeling of not feeling and the darkness of a life becoming tasteless. It's part and parcel with the chronic health issues I've journeyed with for a decade now. When the body shuts down, the mind and heart wrestle with vitality and I find myself unable to give God the affections I deeply long to return to Him.

But I've experienced another cause of spiritual numbness too. The disappointment of unanswered prayer and long-term unmet longings. The reality is, if we keep hoping for something long enough, and life keeps offering us heartbreak in return, the threat of developing a kind of stoic resignation is real. The pain of thirsting becomes unbearable, and we start shutting it down.

Have you ever felt that? Maybe it's trying for a child, or another relationship in the dust as you enter your later years. Careers that implode right at crucial moments or the disappointment of breaking another diet or gym program.

In the face of all that let-down hope, our thirst can become threatening. A force offering us false hope, a promise impossible, a reminder of what isn't. When we're faced with the prospect of all that, it's easier to watch another episode in a series, waste time on reels, or sink ourselves in obsessive activities or events. What is meant to add to our lives becomes a form of escapism, and our longing numbs.

Numbness is our thirst gone sideways, and it's pervasive in our generation. Just trying to stop the bad habits we've got ourselves into isn't enough to push back against the tsunami of thirst-disorientation we face. We need a gospel for it, we need salvation. A salvation, we'll discover, that arrives to us from the very thirsting heart of God. A healing found in God's loving presence.

This is the context in which we experience the intensity of our thirst. A culture that beckons us to give in to whatever we feel, an economy designed to manipulate it to that end, and a numbness that eventuates either from getting what we want and still thirsting, or from the disappointment that we can't seem to get at all that we truly want. It's no wonder we struggle. That we at times feel lost, silently despairing for ourselves, trying to make sense of the drive that compels us.

But the good news is that when we can name a darkness, we can preach more eloquently the light. Desire is the very heart of the gospel, and awakening to it is the beginning of personal renewal.

Because there's another answer to the question of what to do with our thirst: we can allow it to be transformed in God's presence. That may sound cliché or easy to say, but where we're going is toward a tangible practice of doing this in communion with Him for the rest of our lives.

Our thirsts for food, adventure, sex, notoriety, and money are all just our bent-out-of-shape thirst for God. They're our hearing the message of the world that this existential yearning can be satisfied in anything less than Eternity. They're our energy pouring out, unfocused, into far lesser things.

At first it may be hard to believe that satisfaction in God could be the true and beautiful end to these longings. But think about it, have you ever tasted anything on this earth that has satisfied you more than just temporarily? Have you noticed how no matter how good and beautiful a moment is, be it a sunset, a meal, another person, or a song, it never lasts? It always fades, and yet there's something deep within you that longs for that feeling to never leave.

Why? Who told you that? Nothing in this world suggests that living in that feeling, unceasingly, is plausible or possible, and no one who has ever had the world at their fingertips has feigned final satisfaction. What we really want is perfect goodness, living within us, never leaving. This thirst we feel for everything *is* ultimately our thirst for God, because every good thing on earth is designed to be a taste of an eternal reality.

I've heard it said that "the Fathers of the church say that prayer, properly understood, is nothing other than *becoming a longing for God*."[18] That's what we need, a vision for communion that embraces all our desire, transforming it into spiritual vitality and love. What I'm talking about is desire as prayer, as communion.

This attributing, focusing, and giving over all this energy and life to the being of the Trinity is what the gospel is about, it's what we were made for, it's the divine map for a life of everlasting satisfaction. We just have to make sense of all this yearning within us, we need to acknowledge and awaken to it, so that we can begin that journey.

Underneath all this complexity we experience in the world and in ourselves is a Simplicity. A greater, deeper story. One that gathers us up into something graspable, knowable, lovable. It's cosmic. It's personal.

And it revealed itself to me as a young man when I wasn't even searching for it.

Chapter 3

The Yearning

"As soil receives rain
and coastlands the sea,
as lungs receive air
and the body gravity,
so do we receive Your love,
endlessly and naturally,
without choice, debt or fear.
Your love is Reality."

Prayer Vol. 04

We cannot make sense of the ache within us outside its origin in the God who longs even more than we do. All this fire, all this thirst that inhabits our souls is *His* imprint, *His* song. If we want to answer the question of why we thirst the way we do, why we live in a world so predicated on the pursuit of satisfaction and not just functional living, we have to look well beyond ourselves as far back as Genesis and toward eternity past.

Toward the very thirst of God.

For me, though, my encounter with this pursuing God didn't happen in a Bible study, but in the midst of a life crisis. A time when I wasn't even searching for Him. When I was more lost than I'd ever been, and had no true map for the aches of my existence.

I lived my teen years with a tenderhearted but poorly disciplined devotion to God. I loved parties, and to drink too much. Ultimately, my inability to obtain God's moral standards (and a bad break-up which I blamed on Him) led me to give up on the project of knowing God altogether for the pleasures of the world.

Because I'd spent my entire teens quenching my thirst half on God and half on the world, I figured that unchaining my desire on it would be total liberation. After spending my teen years in and out of pubs and taverns playing music instead of sports, I made the gym my new religion. I worked out, ate a strict diet of meat, greens, and protein shakes, and began to live my life entirely for myself. However hard I'd partied as a teen, I did more than all that combined in this short period of my life. I had a broken heart and I sought to fill it with everything I'd felt God had kept me from.

I drank the world in every way I could.

The result was a tragic surprise, I felt even more empty, more lonely, more lost than ever. It turned out that no God was far worse than one with standards I couldn't meet, and even worse, the stuff He'd been protecting me from was a bottomless pit of dissatisfaction anyway. I was living in a kind of disbelieving daze, disappointed, yet unwilling to return to the God I'd left.

Then on the New Year break that same year whilst I was in the middle of a relationship that began on a sticky downtown dance floor in the early hours of the morning, when my life was just one party to the next, God spoke gently to my heart. "Strahan, I love you. Come home to Me." It was a soft whisper, a faint thought. Enough to pass off as a hangover from my "Christian past." But day after day it returned to me quietly, kindly, and without judgement, "Strahan, come home to Me. I love you."

I couldn't deny something was going on. It wasn't just the voice, which felt like my conscience speaking, it was the way it made me feel. Every time it came to me, it was like a warm blanket being wrapped around my heart, it relaxed me, I knew it was Home speaking. I may not have liked the implications, but I couldn't deny the reality: God was pursuing me.

All my teens, I'd tried to please God and yet it was this moment, when I was truly my worst, all walled up in my insecurities, angry, and living my ugliest, railing against His existence, that He chose to show me the extent of His desire for me. None of that seemed to matter to Him, none of my shortfalls and weaknesses, God *wanted* me. Not because I could please Him, my circumstances made that clear, but because He simply did.

I could feel His tender love drawing me back to Him. I still hurt and had plenty of questions, but God's longing felt undeniable. It made sense of my own.

A week later when my casual girlfriend and I reconnected from our separate holidays, I couldn't sleep. I knew I had to say something, to *do* something. I lay there, the Spirit speaking, my heart racing for hours on end until finally a few hours before dawn I woke her up. "I need to tell you something," I staggered nervously, "I'm a Christian." Those words were as much of a shock to myself as they must have been to her.

She wept.

Only a few nights earlier, completely unbeknownst to me, she'd sat hungover on a Fiji beach and made a New Year's resolution herself, a prayer really, "God, if You're out there, I want to get to know You." God had been pursuing us both.

Right there, in the middle of our lostness we discovered just how passionately God longs for us, even in our worst. We woke the next day and committed our lives to Him, then with a whole lot of grit and false starts, our relationship too. Three years later we were married.

We've been together sixteen years since.

And I've never left God again.

Before there was an "us," there was God in what theologians call the Trinity. God the Trinity is a being of community—Father, Son, and Spirit in eternal self-offering love, pouring one another into each other in ecstatic joy, peace, and perfection. He Himself is movement, is living, is a never-ending Conversation of love.

When we think of God, so many of us conjure images of a detached, ethereal Spirit or possibly even an old man sitting on a large throne. But what is more true is a vibrant, passionate, and vital community. Three persons, one essence, all giving themselves fully into the other only to receive the other perfectly and wholly back in unashamed, unhidden love.

Like a waterfall falling into a waterfall, falling into a waterfall, He is literally *the* perfect relationship and it's this relationship we're talking about when we say the word "God."

Think of you and two of your closest friends or family members sharing wine over a good meal at a candlelit table, the deep powerful joy of two parents holding their baby for the first time, a bride and groom at a wedding party, or the first time you made love to your spouse. Take all of those experiences, add them together, and multiply it by eternity and you can begin to touch the nuclear joy and vitality of the unceasing, loving existence of God.

He is living, unadulterated desire.

And He is the most secure Being to ever exist.

Because at the very heart of the Trinity is *agape* love. A love that is selfless, that gives itself away unconditionally. It's precisely in this self-offering that the Father, Son, and Spirit are in-filled and as we'll soon see, that we discover the very key to our existence.

It's difficult to grasp the gravity of this kind of love, but I felt like I got a taste of it, in the tiniest way by comparison, as a younger boy. At primary school I had made it into the interschools cross-country. I was a champion in my own school, but when it came to competition day against the others, I seemed to crumble. It was cold, muddy, rugged, and my asthma was kicking in. For most of the run I was last and feeling humiliated.

I had a hard time finding my place at primary school, I'd hoped placing well at the interschools would give me enough street cred to make a new run of it. Instead I was going to come last by minutes. I wanted to fall into the mud and become one with it. At that age, these things feel like the end of the world.

Then, something happened, I heard heavy breathing behind me. I wasn't last after all. It was the other boy who had qualified from my year. He felt how I felt, he was exhausted and he was crying.

Something came over me when I saw him, a genuine experience of outside of myself compassion. Suddenly, my feelings of humiliation felt less important than his. My heart broke for him. I was going to feel terrible anyway, but he didn't have to. Before we rounded the final bend to the finish line where all the other children, finished, were already standing, I stopped and let him pass me.

As I rounded the bend and crossed the finish line, I could see the look on the other kids' faces when they watched me cross over. They felt sorry for me, it was every kid's worst nightmare. My parents felt sorry for me too, I could see it in their eyes. But the truth was the opposite, I felt true joy. The pain and embarrassment I may otherwise have felt were eclipsed by seeing this other kid from my school not having to wear it.

Instead of feeling sorry for myself, I felt full of love.

That's God. Every moment of every day.

The feeling of that race is still fresh for me today, and yet God has lived in that kind of self-offering wholly receiving abundance eternally.

It's in this nature of other-loving, His giving Himself so freely away, that we begin to touch the "why" of creation. Because that there was ever such a thing as a "beginning" outside of this trinitarian reality is a testimony to something deeper, something more dynamic than a bored deity in need of company, or an insecure one desperate for adulation. Through the Trinity we see creation as a testimony to desire. Because despite His lack or need for us, a story of otherness unfolds in those first few chapters of Genesis. God expresses His longing outward, creatively, passionately, thirsting for more.

That something more is us.

Hidden in this very first line of Scripture we discover the Yearning, the Eternal Thirst. We discover that life as we know it, this world and cosmos we live in, isn't accidental or assumed, but is an act of loving intent by Someone far greater than itself. It had a beginning, it's the product of a Creator, this Being of trinitarian experience.

Life exists because God wants it to.

It may sound understandably foreign to hear the language of thirst when expressing the kind of desire God has for us. We thirst because if we don't drink, we die. But God isn't like that. Paul tells his listeners in Acts 17:24 that "the God who made the world and everything in it, being Lord of heaven and earth, does not live in temples made by man, nor is he served by human hands, as though he needed anything, since he himself gives to all mankind life and breath and everything."

God doesn't need us, that's crucial. But as important, is the often at best minimised and at worst forgotten reality that instead, God wants us. And if God's wanting us isn't based on His need to be glorified, served, or pleased, if it's based on His nature, then it isn't dependent on what we do. We can't make Him desire us any less, or more, than He already does. Because desire is who He is, we have become the glorious beneficiaries of the Trinity's unceasing creative longing. We exist to receive His passionate love.

And God thirsts for us to long for Him in return.

Why not pause for a moment to sit with the gravity of this. You were made from, and for, desire. You are not an accidental child, a servant, or even a subject. You're the object of God's impenetrable affections made to be enjoyed and to enjoy Him forever. Created to drink deeply of His presence. Long before any fall or disorder this was the gospel.

And it still is.

Allow it to move beyond your thoughts, deep down into your soul.

Breathe deeply.

God. Desires. You.

This is the Yearning beneath all creation. The life beneath all life. Not just a friendly love, but a love of passion, beauty, and longing. Or what philosophers and theologians call *eros*.

GOD'S LOVE IS A YEARNING LOVE

I know the word *eros* can conjure some discomfort because it's become so linked with the hyper-eroticism of our culture. If you feel that way, you're not alone, biblical writers and theologians throughout history have felt the same caution. But if you can, just suspend that feeling for a moment as we explore the wonder and beauty of this love that is so much more than the thinly defined sexual romanticism we've relegated it to.

Because it has something to offer us about who God is, who we are, and what we mean when we say He desires.

Yes, Eros was the god of love and sex in Greek mythology. For the Romans, it took the more familiar form of Cupid, often depicted as a baby with a bow and arrow, who when he shoots someone causes them to fall madly in love with the person in front of them. The name Cupid itself, derived from Latin, means "to desire."

But it was the Greek philosopher Plato who first coined the word *eros*, and for him, it meant something much more than romantic love or sexual desire. For Plato, eros was the inherent drive in every human person for goodness, beauty, and truth. A crucial propelling force that drew us into a *more*ness. In his vision, it's our ache for drinking in the beauty of the world and to admire and enjoy what is whole and good.

Think of a rosy-eyed young adult getting access to the world for the first time and the passion they feel for drinking in its culture, vistas, food and wine, and adventure. This is an energetic love of life, the excitement of living. It's art, song, and sex. It's vital and magnetising. Plato saw eros not only as the fire within us for life but an energy drawing us upward, in other words, beyond ourselves.

In Christian theology we can say a wholehearted amen. For us, as one theologian says, "the burning flame of eros speaks of our heart's longing for eternity. It speaks of our destiny."[19] Christians were able to embrace this vision of longing love because they saw it in the human condition, in the biblical story, and in the creative, beautifying heart of God.

Except for us, eros isn't just any old desire pulling us beyond ourselves, nor is it restricted to a sexualised love. It's our ache, our very thirst for God.

Eros, then, isn't only Rolheiser's *dis*-ease, it's our divine homing beacon.

It's the eros in us that appreciates fine art, is moved by songs and poetry, longs for a better world, and for romance, not just transactional sex or platonic relationships. It's not only a sexual force but the turbine that sends us out from our homes as young men and women to conquer our vocation and make a difference in the world. It's a God-given energy, deep within us. A fire, a "burning that can lead either to the torment of pain or the torrent of love," according to one theologian, a power that "will either consume or consummate us."[20]

And it's the image of the One who made us. It springs from the very heart of God Himself. Eros tells us something about the Eternal Yearning and, in doing so, something about where our home is.

Because it's this same God with this loving energy that made the world not just functional, but beautiful. That made sex not just practical and for procreation, but a stunning act of emotional and physical intimacy too. It's this *Eros* that created us with the capacity for music, dance, and the arts. Who gave us imagination and wonder, who filled *us* with desire. Think of Beethoven, Rembrandt, the Palace of Versailles, or the poetry of T. S. Eliot, Emily Dickinson, or Shakespeare. All that creativity and wonder is part of our God-image

That's how beautiful God is.

When we say God wants us, when we talk about God creating us out of desire, this is the kind of desire we're talking about. *This* is the kind of love. And if it makes you feel a little uncomfortable that God loves this way, that He loves *you* this way, you're touching the confronting and often-forgotten, radical, and passionate love of God.

God loves you like a work of art, you are literally His "masterpiece," his "poem," Paul tells us in Ephesians 2:10.[21]

As a teenager I was the only Christian in my friendship group. I was discovering my love for heavy music, spending my nights and weekends rehearsing and playing shows as the lead singer in a rock band. I loved the genre. It had a way of tapping into the angst I felt as a teen finding my place, my anger toward injustice, my passion for life.

But in my later years as I started making Christian friends, I was shocked to discover how sanitised their music was. It was placid and vanilla, theologically correct but emotionally safe. It lacked the edge of the music I listened to. It didn't feel honest to me, it didn't long, it touched nothing of the pain in me for healing and love.

Sure, it was loving and it was true, but not *wholly* true. It was full of the right language and moral propositions, but it was so safe that it felt nothing like the God I knew, who entered humanity's mess, felt our pain, lived on our streets, and experienced our parties.

It lacked real beauty, passion, *eros.*

And how sadly true is it that our spirituality can be the same. One that's true but not risky, loving but not pursing, feeling but not aching, obeying but not pining, drinking but not thirsting. That's what a faith without eros gets you. One that looks more like Ned Flanders than Jesus. And a God who can't understand our raw longing, because He's a Ned Flanders too.

Importantly, there's a vital difference between the eros common in our world (and of the Greeks' envisioning) and the eros that is God's. In God, the Eternal Yearning, we find the perfect tension between eros and agape love. If eros is the passionate seeking of love, beauty, and drinking the other, agape is the selfless, serving love that stops it from turning inward on itself in what the monastics call the lust of man. For the desert fathers and mothers, lust wasn't just about selfish sexual desire but the general desire to use the world, material possessions, and others, for self gain.

The kind of eros God is, is the opposite. The way God pursues us is through self-sacrifice and co-suffering. God is eros and agape in perfect tension. Beautifying the other for their good, longing not only to satisfy His longing for us but our longing for love simultaneously. A Trinitarian desire.

GOD THIRSTS

This beautifying, desiring Christ is the one who stands in the middle of the feast of our lives and the marketplace of our wants and disorientations seeking to be loved, seeking to be wanted by us. If you've ever risked telling someone you love them, you'll have a taste of how Jesus must have felt that day. There as He declares His longing to be longed for, He makes Himself profoundly available and vulnerable, hoping for our response.

This is why fourth-century theologian and doctor of desire Saint Augustine could say, "God thirsts that we would thirst for Him."[22] In Christ, Augustine saw God's longing living among us, walking our streets, laying all His cards out on the table.

Notice that when Jesus does invite us to come and drink, He doesn't just quietly murmur His invitation among a few close friends, He stands up in the middle of our partying and "cries out," which could equally be translated as "to scream" or "shout." It's a passionate plea, a calling, something much deeper than cold public discourse.

Awakening to God's longing, and His vulnerability in revealing it to us, has had a transformative effect on me in these years. It's made me want to make so much more of myself available to Him. It's changed how I understand prayer, and how I live toward Him. It's not the image of God I formed as a young man. This God who is grieved by our rejection of Him not only because it's "wrong," as true as that is, but because it deprives Him of His drinking of us too. It deprives Him of His union with us.

For some, that may be a hard image to grasp. God may be more distant than that, too sanitised, too rigid. But time and time again in Scripture, God risks it all to show us He wants us for this very reason, if we're willing to feel the stories we read and not only intellectualise them.

It may not be in the same way we do, without insecurity and need, but God desires, He thirsts.

IN GOD'S IMAGE

When we look at the God of eros-agape, this trinitarian God who creates out of the longing of love, we not only discover who He really is, but who *we* are as well. Because it's this God who said, "Let us make man in our image,"[23] and it's here that our powerful and bottomless thirst begins to make sense.

I am not made in the image of some passive, gentle love, but of this passionate, beautifying, and vivifying love that pursues, romanticises, and longs for union with the object of its affection. If God is a community of love that empties Himself into the other only to be filled perfectly to the very core by Himself, and I'm made in *that* image, then the true depth of my need reveals itself to me as something profoundly divine.

Now I'm free to see that the source of my hydration can never be this world with its sex, food and drink, career, influence and notoriety. The blueprint of my thirst is eternal and it will only be in Eternity that it's fully satisfied. If I don't drink of *this* love, I'm empty.

Finally I can stop trying to engulf the world so ravenously. I can say to all my detoured desires, "*You're* not what I want, I want *Love!*" and turn my attention toward the Divine One who truly can fulfil.

Suddenly, all my aches and wants have a place to return to, a *telos* to direct themselves toward.

Now Jesus' statement "If you're thirsty, come and drink" becomes real. Prayer becomes not a place to go to placate God's demands but a place of divine pleasure, of desire, of the deepest kind of love and want. A place to go to learn to drink, to relent to God's desire to know me. A place to open up and be seen.

Our thirst isn't a result of the fall, it's by design. Our *dis*-ease is in-built. Desire isn't a problem to be fixed but a power to be harnessed to propel us toward Love. That's not to say that any desire we feel is suddenly okay. We suffer a confusion, a disorder, as a result of our brokenness and this broken world. Something we'll explore later, in the "Discerning Movements" chapter.

But it does mean that we shouldn't be afraid to get in touch with our deepest longings, nor to allow ourselves to believe that, even more than we long for anything in this life, God longs for us, and longs for us to long for Him.

Like God pursued me that summer, He pursues the world, and us, now. He's not interested in some platonic arrangement. He's not looking for servants who are only interested in right and wrong. He wants to hydrate our souls, to live there, beautifying and singing in the heart of our deepest self.

God longs to marry us.

Chapter 4

A Thirst of God

"Christ hides Himself away,
buried in the plain sight
of our hearts and lives,
longing to be longed for,
aching to be the Treasure
that we sell all we have to find."

Prayer Vol. 04

On September 10, 1946, a young Catholic nun named Agnes Bojaxhiu was sitting on a train, heading for her annual retreat in Darjeeling, when she had a life-altering, mystical experience. As she prayed, she had a vision of Jesus on the cross crying the words "I thirst." Captivated by the pain and longing, she felt His aching love, His want for more than just drink. What Agnes saw that day on the train was God's eternal, passionate thirst for human souls.

The encounter shaped the direction of the rest of her life. She soon left her position as a Catholic school headmistress and sought to quench God's thirst for souls amidst the world's most poor. Energised by her revelation of divine desire, her movement the Missionaries of Charity would go on to found houses around the world, inspire over 4,000 sisters to join its order, and plant 610 foundations in 123 countries with its mantra to "satiate the thirst of Jesus on the Cross for love of souls."[24]

Her vision had caught on, and she became one of the most globally recognised saints of the twentieth century. Known affectionately to so many of us as Mother Teresa of Calcutta.

Mother Teresa would later write letters to the Missionaries of Charity imploring them to know and experience the passionate love God had for each of them. A mystic at heart, the very centre of her energy for seeking justice for the poor was expressed in her encouragement to the Charity: "'I thirst' is something much deeper than Jesus just saying 'I love you.' Until you know deep inside that Jesus thirsts for you—you can't begin to know who He wants to be for you. Or who He wants you to be for Him."[25]

Teresa saw something vital in Jesus' love, something deeper, something more overwhelming. She saw what I experienced myself that summer years ago, His thirst. A thirst for something far greater than friendship or proximity, a thirst to become one with our very souls. A union comparable to only one thing on earth, marriage.

FROM DISCIPLE, TO CHILD, TO LOVER

The image of marriage as a way for understanding salvation, and prayer, makes many people uncomfortable. Especially Protestants, and especially in today's world so sexualised and corrupted by the use of domination that it's hard to think of marriage through anything other than those unappealing frames. But I hope to show you that marriage, with its naked vulnerability, compassionate acceptance, and unique sense of *in*ness, is a vital biblical refrain used for communion not only by the Bible's authors, but God Himself. One that may change everything about how we pray.

So, stay with me as we spend this chapter briefly exploring the greatest love story of all time.

In the arc of the New Testament, from Jesus' life through to Revelation, we see an invitation to continually move deeper in Love.

The Gospels begin with Jesus inviting us to "come, follow." This invitation is pivotal in our lives. It takes us from being strangers to being in the proximity of God Himself. The call to follow is a call to become Jesus' apprentice. An apprentice has a teacher, and in Christ we find a *loving* Teacher. Someone who will gently guide us in the right way to live justly in this world, knowing and delighting in God as we were made to.

We never cease being a disciple, of course, but it's not the only relational framework between God and us offered in the Scriptures. If we only think of ourselves as disciples we could be forgiven for living in a sort of *adjacent* paradigm with Jesus, lovingly working together, but never truly risking vulnerability and seenness. A disciple is close, but maybe not that close. And it is close that God truly wants.

And so we read in John 15:15 that Jesus tells the disciples, "I no longer call you servants ... I have called you friends." Friendship is altogether different than the student-teacher relationship. They share more than just work and ethics with one another, they share their lives. Friends can relax, they can *be* together, even when they're not learning. In fact, friends are defined by spending their downtime together far more than their work.

Friends waste time together, they laugh, open up, and share their hearts. Ultimately, friends are at rest in each other's presence, they enjoy *being* together. Jesus telling the disciples they were friends didn't override their identity as disciples, it informed and shaped it. The kind of discipleship we experience in Christ involves our being as well as our doing. But it doesn't end there.

Later in the New Testament Paul takes divine proximity even further, calling us "*children* of God." To be God's child is to be something even more vulnerable and dependent than a friend. It's to be secure in our identity as His, to know that we are already and will continue to inherit everything of His kingdom and eternal life. It speaks to our rebirth, our new-creationness. As God's children we're even more secure than friends, and invited to a very different kind of conversation than a classic disciple would ever encounter.

Again, being a child of God doesn't mean we're not friends or disciples. What we're seeing is the deepening and development of our identity, not a replacement of titles. Each informing the other. Think of it like looking at something in one, two, or three dimensions. Each perspective is true of the object and never changes it, but it does change the way we understand and experience the object as a whole. Likewise each progression of identity builds on the next. A continual movement towards a richer intimacy. Each one more bold than the last.

Then finally, in Revelation 22, we're confronted with the pinnacle of the divine story and our deepest vocation. There we hear the aching prayer that has inhabited history since Pentecost, a prayer of anticipation, beckoning the return of Christ and the healing of creation, "The Spirit and the *Bride* say, 'Come.'"[26] The deepest cry of God's people coming not from a school of students, a group of friends, or a nation of children but from the aching longing of a *spouse*, yearning for final union with its Love.

The ultimate journey into God, this prayer in Revelation suggests, is the journey into spousal love. Consummating every image and identifier we find of our relationship to God in the New Testament, this is our *telos*. This level of oneness. A revelation that begins with God's thirst for us and ends with our resounding *yes*.

If you're counting words, the church as the bride of God isn't the most common theme for our identity in the New Testament. "Disciple" and "child" are used significantly more. But it is the most intimate one, providing a scandalous insight not only into who we are, but into the very heart of God Himself.

YOUR MAKER IS YOUR HUSBAND

Few images in Scripture are more proactive than God as Bridegroom. For many, knowing God as "Father" is a significant enough leap for those who feel Him to be aloof and unknowable, let alone Husband. And yet, if speaking of God as spouse or lover is borderline, no one told the prophets. Nor the writers of the New Testament. The imagery of God as spouse is central to the biblical story.

In the Gospels, John the Baptist referred to himself as the "friend of the bridegroom,"[27] and Jesus called Himself the bridegroom in His teaching on fasting in Mark 2:19 and in the parables in Matthew 22 and 25. When He does, His listeners don't bat an eyelid. Of the many of Jesus' teachings that offended the religious leaders of His time, that of God's desire to marry humanity wasn't one of them. That's because for Israel, God as husband wasn't only *a* theme, but a dominant one.

Long before Jesus' ministry, God in a stunning declaration through the prophet Isaiah proclaims to Israel, "Your Maker is your husband." Not in a formal or contractual way either, but a personal, tender one. "As a bridegroom rejoices over his bride," we're told, "so will your God rejoice over you."[28] This is no off-the-cuff remark, this is an astounding revelation of how God feels about humanity that continues as a motif throughout the prophetic tradition.

The whole prophetic book of Hosea uses the imagery of God as husband to Israel, saying, "I will betroth you to me forever. I will betroth you to me in righteousness and in justice, in steadfast love and in mercy," and again, "'In that day,' declares the LORD, 'you will call me "my husband"; you will no longer call me "my master.""""[29] In Hosea we discover God's deep displeasure with the way our relationship was defined, and His desire to transform it miraculously.

This story of God's desire for humanity and our wayward heart is a continuous refrain throughout the prophets. In fact, Old Testament idolatry (the worship of other gods) was regularly lamented not so much as the breaking of the law, but as adultery.

"You have committed *adultery* on every high mountain," God tells Israel through Isaiah. "There you have worshiped idols and have been *unfaithful* to me."[30] Worshiping other gods is infidelity, because salvation is a story of a loving union, not servitude or obedience. This personalises sin profoundly, makes it relational, and gives us a glimpse into the loving vulnerability of God.

We may not find ourselves today tempted to worship Baal, Molech, or Ra like the Ancient Near East, but the world with its sex, materialism, power, and wealth tempts us all the same. The early church felt this too, which is why James was quick to remind them of this relational, spousal dimension to double-living, "You *adulterous* people, don't you know that friendship with the world means enmity against God?"[31]

Dabbling in the world, James would say, is cheating on God. We cannot have two spouses. We are either God's or the world's.

And what kind of husband does God long to be for us? We get a glimpse through the prophet Ezekiel:

> Later I passed by, and when I looked at you and saw that you were old enough for love, I spread

the corner of my garment over you and covered
your naked body. I gave you my solemn oath and
entered into a covenant with you, declares the
Sovereign LORD, and you became mine.

I bathed you with water and washed the blood
from you and put ointments on you. I clothed
you with an embroidered dress and put sandals of
fine leather on you. I dressed you in fine linen and
covered you with costly garments. I adorned you
with jewellery: I put bracelets on your arms and
a necklace around your neck, and I put a ring on
your nose, earrings on your ears and a beautiful
crown on your head. So you were adorned with
gold and silver; your clothes were of fine linen and
costly fabric and embroidered cloth. Your food was
honey, olive oil and the finest flour. You became
very beautiful and rose to be a queen. And your
fame spread among the nations on account of your
beauty, because the splendour I had given you
made your beauty perfect, declares the Sovereign
LORD.[32]

This language is scandalous. Listen to the way God speaks of us,
how dangerous He's willing to be. If there are any nerves about this
imagery, they're not on God's end of the conversation. This is the
language of love, of eros, of desire. God adorns the prize of His affection with jewels and gifts, beautifying her and lavishing her with the

riches of heaven. This is the language of One who wants to be more than Lord, God to us. It's One who longs to be *Beloved*.

God beautifies the objects of His affection. That's what He longs to do for each and every one of us. Salvation isn't only a transaction in which sin is removed and a debt cleared, it's God's promise to dress us in goodness, gentleness, joy, truth, and peace. To clothe us in what *He's* clothed in, to make us like Him through His desire and grace.

For the apostle Paul, human marriage is a prophecy, a sign of this incomprehensible, personal miracle. Quoting Genesis he says, "For this reason a man will leave his father and mother and be united to his wife, and the two will become one flesh. This is a profound mystery—but I am talking about Christ and the church."[33]

This is a statement about the church wider as Christ's body. It's also, as we'll see soon, about what it truly means to be filled with the Spirit as individuals. God became human in Jesus Christ, not only for a moment, but for eternity, so that in Him we, too, may for eternity be married to God.

Take a slow, deep breath.

Let it sink beyond your mind into your heart.

You are God's beloved.

Shortly after Katie and I decided to respond to God's loving invitation, that New Year she moved back down to Dunedin in the far south of Aotearoa to finish her study. We'd only just committed to turning our personal lives around, and now, in the midst of all that disorientation, we were trying to build a godly relationship three hours' flight from each other.

For two years we worked through becoming new people, living a long-distance relationship, and navigating all the highs and vulnerabilities of young love. We laughed, longed, fought, broke up, got back together, laughed some more, broke up again, worked it through, grew, and loved each other.

But the biggest test of our love was a few months before she came back to Auckland, when deep down I knew it was time to take the ultimate risk and to ask her to marry me. Knowing each other wasn't enough anymore. Being close friends was great, being romantic friends was even better. But I wanted more. I wanted to make it exclusive, to spend the rest of our lives together, to become one.

That meant asking her to marry me, and that meant a whole new self-exposure, the kind of which I'd never experienced before. Because marriage isn't only about how much you love someone, it's about how much of yourself you give away too.

There is a real vulnerability to being in love. With anyone else we can be detached, colder, more calculated. But when we're in love, the compass spins. We want to open up to the object of our affection, but the prospect of that openness being misused or uncared for is pathologically terrifying. But there comes a time in the midst of all that reckoning with knowing and sharing hearts that a penny drops and we realise that we want to continue this open-heart surgery with this person for the rest of our lives. Why? Because, like Katie and I, we want to be *more* than a romantic interest to our love, we want to live in an emotional and physical union.

Marriage, truly understood, isn't the end of the journey of romance, but the beginning of it. It consummates love by creating a safety net, a promise to stay and to *see* the other when we're afraid that, deep down, we're unlovable. It's this seeing, emotionally, mentally, physically, this fearless nakedness with this one person, that comes to define the rest of our lives.

And despite it invoking a degree of inter-knowing that makes many of us recoil, that's precisely the kind of union God longs to have with us. A Spirit-to-soul baring all in a fearless openness.

Tragically, we tend to prefer the God who is so holy we can't be intimate, so grand that He's not heart-close. Subconsciously, I think we feel it might protect us, because opening ourselves to this kind of intimacy with God threatens the very walls within us we've built to keep ourselves safe. If God truly sees us, we may too, and most of us have things within us we've spent our lives consciously or unconsciously ignoring.

I wonder if when Mother Teresa said, "Until you know deep inside that Jesus thirsts for you—you can't begin to know who He wants to be for you,"[34] this consummating love was where her spirit was taking her. To this place of deep communion where God thirsts to be with us, in full self-disclosure, in the sharing of our deepest selves.

This Yearning is the beating heart beneath all living. Not a God who would have subjects, disciples, or even just friends (as great as those are!), but One who would have us as *lovers*. To know and be known by Him even more fully than any earthly spouse.

Thirsting, then, is an unavoidable journey toward divine vulnerability. Toward naked-being, and a willingness to feel the risk, and go there anyway, with God.

God's language of spousal love draws us toward this kind of trust. To the kind of union that takes us beyond just the way we act and think about God into the opening up of our very inner movements—our desires, longings, and displacements. Spousal love refuses to let the soul be untouched by the Yearning. It wants intimacy more than self-preservation.

Because when we allow Love to heal us in these places, at the level of our deepest vulnerabilities, we heal the root of the tree. Every flailing branch and withering leaf is reborn when love touches our most deeply rooted brokenness, the brokenness at the level of our desires. But to allow God in like that, we need to live in vulnerability.

A vulnerability that flies in the face of the hyper-individualised, self-sufficiency of our times.

EMBRACING INSUFFICIENCY

Sin, and the hurts of this world, have taught us to try to be enough for ourselves. To be independent emotionally, spiritually, and mentally. We live in a culture where being an individual is idolised above all else and the "self-made" woman or man is the mythical hero of many of our rags-to-riches stories.

But we were never made to be independent and self-sufficient. "It's not good for man to be alone,"[35] remember? In fact, the Scriptures call the vision for self-sufficiency "pride," the greatest inhibitor to communion with God.

In God the Trinity we see a community of being inseparably united in love to one another, and it's into that other-dependency that humanity is invited to participate. Dependence isn't weakness, it's holiness.

But what happens in our living is we build defence mechanisms to cope with our being hurt, rejected, left alone, or under threat by the lack of love in others. We individualise our souls as a survival mechanism. It's cold out here, the world isn't a place for raw vulnerability. Soft-hearted people get used. We're all afraid.

We convince ourselves that self-sufficiency is possible. That we can heal ourselves. That we're better off looking out for number one, not letting even God any closer. We assume that we're meant to be able to stand alone and to never suffer the feelings of vulnerability that make us so deeply uncomfortable. But entering that space is precisely what communion is.

Our insufficiency is a gift meant to draw us back to the spousal love of God. We are only complete when in union with Him. Only our truest selves when we are our beloved selves.

For that reason, the project of individualism doesn't work. It only makes us more numb, more hidden from who we really are, and more unable to experience the piercing, jubilant love of God in the depth of us. The goal of the Christian life isn't to become more self-sufficient using the teaching Jesus gave us, but to become more joyfully and tenderly dependent. To awaken to the beauty of being completed in union with God.

Few places expose the risk of this kind of holy living than in the place of our pain. Where the world would have us insulate ourselves from suffering by keeping people away, God's spousal love invites us to instead bare all and trust Him. To let Him be our balm, to believe that He's loving, that He cares, and that He's enough.

Opening up to God where we're strong costs nothing, opening up in our greatest weaknesses, is faith. Ultimately, I believe that's what the vision of God as spouse, rather than disciple or friend, reveals to us. A bare-all, intermingling of being, vulnerable, and other-sufficient union. It's an invitation to such radical faith as to believe that God can be the perfect lover. That, in Him, it's possible to make ourselves both more vulnerable and more secure simultaneously.

And how can we know this for sure? How can we know that vulnerability and availability are at the very heart of God's spousal love for us? Because God went there first. The greatest act of vulnerable, other-love is Jesus Christ hanging on a cross for us. Jesus' *love through death* shows us that there can be no experiencing the heights of love, without the pain of facing shame and guilt.

On the cross, God doesn't run from pain, shame, or risk but expresses His love perfectly through it. There in the chaos created by our self-sufficiency and in the midst of our wayward hearts He cries out for us, arms nailed wide open, the Yearning cries to us, "I thirst."[36]

Yes, He was physically dehydrated, but perhaps too it was a pro-phetic cry. Perhaps here we discover a Love who identifies with the psalmists, crying out in their longing for God centuries before. One who knows exactly what we feel in our own spiritual dehydration.

Perhaps there in His last moments, God was expressing solidar-ity with you, with me, saying that He knows exactly what it's like to put yourself out there and risk rejection. To know what it's like to become vulnerable, to risk love in the hope of being loved back.

Perhaps, too, in our rejection of Him there, He experienced the pain of love more than you and I could ever imagine. Perhaps in that way He made living in the risky ache of divine vulnerability a shared experience, showing us that He knows what it's like to be unsure, that He understands our fear of fully opening up and being seen.

Marriage to God is provocative and confronting. Understood as the deepest place of loving intimacy in the identities of the New Testament, it reveals the longing at the very centre of God's heart, His longing to be exclusively ours, to know us in our deepest places, for us to be vulnerable and available to Him.

And just like human marriage, it involves a journey *in* to one another. Only, where human union is limited to the body, the gift of God's life to us goes so much further, into an experience of His Spirit in the very seat of our being. Through Jesus, we're invited into a whole new experience of the Yearning.

We're invited into the *Conversation*.

"Come to Me"

You were longing for me,
wanting for deeper places,
unaccepting of my shallows,
You beckoned, a whisper,
opening an ocean in me
that we might both sink in.

Chapter 5

Divine Conversing

"Let me be among You
as You are among You."
Prayer Vol. 02

Have you ever had the experience in which, standing before a grand vista or listening to a powerful song, you just wanted to be *in* it? By "in" it, I mean that you wanted to consume more of it somehow, get it right down into your bones. Or maybe that's exactly how it did feel. Music has always done that for me, especially when I was younger.

Music has a mystical ability to reach right down into my soul and grab hold of it. As if, for the few minutes I'm immersed in it, it *has* me, consumes me, speaks to my truest longings. For a moment I feel myself becoming my uninhibited self.

I've been at concerts and seen this very same experience in others as they've wept, looking calmly possessed by the kind of joy and heart-grabbedness that I feel when I play. Nothing speaks to me of the human capacity for finding the ache within us more than the intense connection that happens through music.

Creation can do the same too. On a perfect day when the ocean beach outside our home is coloured crystal green and blue, I get a transcendent feeling of wanting to drink the whole thing in. Not with a physical thirst, but an eros one. Seeing it just doesn't feel like enough. I want us to be one.

This impulse that makes us want to consume beauty, to be a part of it permanently, hints at what we were made for. Our pining for *in*ness, our wanting to be grabbed hold of in the very seat of us, comes out of our divine identity as beloved. It speaks to what our end is. God made art, love and sex, creation, and beauty as gifts for us to enjoy, as foretastes of our ultimate longing. As an entrée. Something tangible to tease the Greater Gift.

This longing-space God put in us is for Himself.

His invitation to make us His home.

Before Jesus was crucified, He made His disciples, and us, a profound promise, "on that day you will realise that I am in my Father, and you are in me, and I am in you."[37] *In* you. *In* me. Jesus tells us that He's going to consummate our shared longing for satisfying intimacy, to finish the work of meeting our existential thirst. To be the song that grips us, the vista that swallows us up. To experience the Trinity in and through Him. To indwell us.

But what is that experience like, exactly?

Almost three-quarters of the earth's surface is covered by ocean, yet we've only explored 5 percent of what's within it. Until a few decades ago we knew more about the surface of the moon than we did about the ocean's greatest depths. To us, its dark and high-pressured world is a mystery untapped.

Is it possible that, spiritually speaking, we're the same? Living from the surface of ourselves, largely unaware of the wonder within. Because our world is a litany of surface living, now more than ever thanks to the ubiquity of access globalisation has brought us, it's possible to live our entire lives as if there were no deep ocean in us at all. No ancient story than the one we're thinly living.

We can spend every minute scrolling, shopping, listening, or doing almost whatever we want, without ever really needing to consider what's going on beneath us. We forget we're souls and what it feels like to simply exist. We lose our sense of even having an "in," and with it, the very place we're made to commune with God.

Origen of Alexandria, a third-century scholar, theologian, and ascetic, using another metaphor, encouraged us, "Understand that you have within yourself, upon a small scale, a second universe; within you there is a sun, there is a moon, and there are also stars."[38] For him, our inner self is a complex, beautiful, and largely unexplored wonder. Many other saints and great pray-ers over history have also considered the soul a thing of great beauty and complexity. Something to be appreciated and studied precisely because it's the world in which God longs to home Himself.

We are, all of us, a mystery. A space made to be filled with the wonder, love, and glory of God. But do we know it? Are we in touch at all with the vastness that is our inner being?

Just like the ocean, we have an unplunged depth to us, a place to find God, a place of darkness. Down there, where the pressure is high and the light of our surface living is dimmed, lies what makes us, *us*—the conscious, the unconscious, the healed and broken, and most importantly, the life of the Spirit.

This "darkness" isn't an evil, but a mystery. Psalm 18:11 tells us, for example, that God "made darkness his covering, his canopy around him," and another declares of Him "even the darkness is not dark to you."[39] The image of darkness isn't one of forbode or fear, but of hiddenness and unknowing.

The psalmists seemed highly self-aware of their inner mystery and the deep tides and caverns that moved below their consciousness. Their response was to speak to their Dark Ocean, calling it up into God: "Why, my soul, are you downcast? ... Put your hope in God" and "Praise the LORD, O my soul. Do not forget all his kind deeds."[40] Long before modern concepts of mindfulness, God's praying people have spoken to their depth, thought about their thoughts, and sought to bring their being into alignment with Reality.

The journey of drinking deeply of God's love begins here with our own awakening to the magnitude of us and with a psalmic awareness that there are uninhabited spaces in us that long to be given over to God. Much of our not noticing the Spirit's movements comes not from His absence, but from our surface living. From our not appreciating, nor living from, the gift of our inner self.

If we're not in touch with this Dark Ocean, and if we refuse to pay attention to what's there and how it moves our conscious living, we'll find ourselves blind to the gift of God's permanent homedness in us too. How can we live with God in a home we don't even acknowledge?

The healthiest human relationships are built on two self-aware people able to bring their whole selves compassionately to the table. When one refuses to face the currents beneath them, driving their malfunction, their lack of awareness keeps them from loving, and being loved, more deeply. Instead, they live at the mercy of their pain and undiagnosed aches.

When we ignore our Dark Ocean, we risk being the same with God. If we don't pray like the psalmists—aware of our inner depth, longings, emotions, hurts, and even lifelessness—we'll hardly know the true power of the hope we're inviting. Or the intimacy. And we'll struggle to know how God's living *in* us transforms our communion.

God longs for and has made a way to live in *us*, not somewhere else. God Himself brought us into the picture, created us, dignified us, made us part of His story, and when it comes to His life within us, if we don't become familiar with the movements of us in our deep places, we won't get to experience the joy and wonder of Him.

The more of our Dark Ocean we can know and appreciate, the more deeply we can experience the beauty and loving presence of God.

When Jesus promises that we'll be in Him and He in us, He's talking about so much more than a one-and-done theological transition. He's talking about an interrelating, an intermingling. It's an invitation to a "Spirit of God encountering human soul" experience.

The promise to be caught up in the Divine Conversation Himself.

THE CONVERSATION

This "being *in* one anotherness" that Jesus promises makes our bodies, our very beings, God's home. It's a Spirit-to-soul personal mingling of selves. The New Testament writers call it our becoming "God's temple," our becoming "one" with Him.[41]

If you've been a Christian for some time, that language may be overly familiar to you, so it can be easy to forget just how radical a statement that truly is. Consider that this is the trinitarian God of all power, mystery, vital love, and creative energy we explored in "The Yearning" chapter. The one who shapes the cosmos, raises the dead, parts oceans, and sees and knows all without strain or lack. This God, who for millennia was only found on mountain tops by the few, experienced by gifted prophets, and met in the most secret place in the temple where one priest could enter once a year, now lives in you and me.

Not in some static, impersonal way either. Because in and through Christ we're invited to experience the Trinity in dynamic, vital community.

In John 1:1, when the apostle began his gospel with "In the beginning was the Word," he was offering some hints to what it means to be *in* God. The original Greek for "Word" here is *logos*, which has a rich meaning that many English translations obscure. When you or I think of a "word," we picture something static, set, like a single arrangement of letters that means something definitive. But *logos* has a fuller meaning than that, stretching to the very act of speaking itself.[42]

In fact, until the fourth century, most translators translated the word *logos* not into English but into Latin, where they used the word *sermo*. *Sermo* is where we get our word *sermon* from[43] and actually means something closer to "discourse," implying a back-and-forth in dialogue.

Going even deeper, the root of *sermo* is *sero*, which is a weaving and a joining, the "intimate living of life together, living among, and all in intimate conversation," as one writer put it.[44] So it seems that the earlier translators of the gospel of John saw something deeply relational in *logos*, one may even say Trinitarian, implied in the opening line.

In light of all this, sixteenth-century scholar Erasmus translated the opening of John's gospel as "In the beginning was the *conversation*."[45]

And what is that conversation? It's the vibrant community of insatiable and other-love we explored in the Yearning. The ever-giving, ever-receiving experience of the Father, Son, and Holy Spirit. A community of love. God has been in dialogue within Himself, in an inexpressible yet vital language from eternity past.

When Jesus says, "On that day you will realise that I am in my Father, and you are in me, and I am in you,"[46] He's not just being poetic, He's speaking of catching us up into *this* dynamic dialogue of holy love and desire. A living, moving reality whether we're awake or asleep, conscious of it or not. Our Dark Ocean being the home of God isn't a static reality, it's our hosting the loving conversation taking place between Father, Son, and Spirit in our very selves.

We are cohabited by the living God.

But there's more, because shortly after Jesus promises a communion of *in*ness with Him, He describes something of the shape it takes when He says, "As the Father has loved me, so have I loved you."[47] Consider that. This is the eternal Word, He who was with God since the beginning, enjoying this trinitarian community of perfect love. Jesus has never been insecure, He's only ever experienced God's joyful love lavished on Him, His affection and peace covering and filling Him, His provision and care looking after Him.

It's impossible for us to imagine what that's like.

And yet now He's saying that He loves us with *that* same love?

There's no thinking our way into grasping the sheer magnitude of this. It must be *experienced*, or better said, co-experienced. This seating of God within us is our entering into the eternal conversation of love through Christ. No longer as an outsider, but an insider. That's what the New Testament language of being "in Christ" is pointing to. Now that we are in Christ, we're invited to experience God as He does.

Or in the language of Paul in Ephesians 1:3, "Jesus Christ ... has blessed us in the heavenly realms with every spiritual blessing in Christ." Everything of God's is ours now, through the life and love of His Son, Jesus. When God says He's living *in* us, this is what He means.

Why not pause again for a moment to truly *feel* that.

In deep breaths.

God loves me. He lives *in* me. I have all of Him.

Know it in the very centre of your being.

Welcome to your Dark Ocean.

It really is too much to take in. Perhaps this was why Paul continually prayed for the church to *experience* the height, depth, length, and breadth of God's love, a love that transcends our ability to rationalise it.[48] Because it can only be known here in our deep self and not in the limitations of our mind. We will never, in this life, understand all this. We can only experience it—the exploration of which is the single greatest invitation of our existence. Salvation isn't only the forgiveness and healing of sin, it's an invitation to this kind of living. To union with God.

This is the way God fulfills His thirst for us, by uniting Himself to us in our *deep self.* There, not only does He begin to satisfy our desire for Him, but through the Spirit He invites us to experience God's desire for God. He becomes the thirst beneath our thirsts. We awaken to divine desire.

We can receive a deep and powerful peace from knowing this. Because on the many days when our love is cold, when our minds are foggy and we're out of strength, all we need to do is quieten ourselves down, return to the revelation of God's life within us, and seek to hear inwardly *His* thirst, *His* love. Then, allowing it to fill our being, we discover our own. We respond to the thirst of God.

At all times, this conversation is going on within us. It's incredible how we continue to go on with our lives as if that's not true. What would it be like if we all suddenly believed it and lived this way? What sense of God's presence would we carry with us, the security, the rested trust? We wouldn't only long for God with His Spirit, but we'd become wells of life to the world around us.

Imagine if we were to spend the first ten minutes of our days simply reminding, awakening to, and experiencing this reality within us. Closing our eyes, holding our coffee or lying in our beds, simply beholding this conversation of love we're now a part of.

That's what it means to receive the thirst of God.

And to begin to satisfy ours in Him.

You're invited to a living, dynamic inter-knowing in the very seat of your soul whether you're conscious of it or not. You only need to say *yes*.

ENCOUNTERING THE FACE OF THE DEEP

Through the gift of the Spirit, we've been invited into a whole new seeing of each other. A beholding, a face-to-faceness prophesied since the days of the Exodus.

So often we look outward for the presence of God, being more attracted to the healings, miracles, and the signs and wonders we read about in the Scriptures. But all of those external things are pointers, road signs toward this greatest miracle of God's love becoming our very inner life. Yes, they're absolutely a crucial aspect of the kingdom of heaven, but they're not the greatest ones.

In the world to come there'll be no need for miracles, signs, and wonders. All that will be left is what's already begun *in* us here, this union with God. Jesus calls this eternal life when He says, "Now this is eternal life: that they know you, the only true God, and Jesus Christ, whom you have sent."[49]

Did you catch that? Jesus says that knowing God, and by implication becoming His home, *is* eternal life. It's not some post-death experience or "get it later" promise, it's life in God today. Signs and wonders will cease, but not this greatest miracle. The greatest miracles aren't so much the dead being raised or lepers healed, it's people like you and me becoming the home of God, becoming one with Him through the gift of His Spirit.

A whole new face-to-faceness.

When it comes to signs and wonders and people close to God, most look no further than Moses. Moses saw God in the burning bush, lived the Exodus miracles, met with angels on the mountain where he received the Commandments, and helped found the nation of Israel.

When the Bible talks of Moses' relationship to God, it says he met with Him "face to face." That's not a statement about human appendages, but of relationship, of intimacy. Our faces, and in particular our eyes, are where we see and are seen by others. They're a window into our inner life, to who we really are. To turn and face someone is to give them time and space. To share our face with another through a kiss is an exclusive sign of trust and intimacy.

Biblically, the face is representative of the whole, personal self. So when God invites us to "seek his face" He means Him, personally in vulnerable totality, not just some aspect of Him like His "outstretched arm" which is illustrative more of His actions.[50] Alternatively to hide one's face is to hide one's self, which is exactly what Moses does when he first encounters God in the burning bush. He "hid his face," we read, "because he was afraid to look at God."[51]

But later in Moses' story, things are different. Because in Numbers 12:6–8, we hear God say:

> When there is a prophet among you,
>> I, the LORD, reveal myself to them in visions,
>> I speak to them in dreams.
> But this is not true of my servant Moses;
>> he is faithful in all my house.
> With him I speak face to face,
>> clearly and not in riddles;
>> he sees the form of the LORD.

Notice the difference between Moses and all other prophets. There's no hiddenness in the way God speaks to him, only honesty, clarity, friendship. Visions, dreams, even burning bushes are great. But they're still the little league. They're obscure, parabolic, and guarded. The real stuff, according to God, is He and us speaking to each other plainly and openly, as friends like He did with Moses.

Yet, we have something greater than Moses.

Moses met with God face to face on a mountain. He experienced Him in thunder and lightning, in cloud and through angels.[52] But now our Dark Ocean is the mountain top, our self the cloud around it, and there are no more mediators, only the Holy Spirit speaking directly to us from within. We don't just see God out there in a burning bush, we have *become* the burning bush.

Deep calling to deep.

Through the Spirit, the face of our deep is now exposed and liberated toward God. Prayer becomes about sinking beneath our surface living to gaze upon God here, in our deep self as He gazes lovingly back. Rather than ascending Mount Sinai we descend into His presence within, braving being naked there, living amidst the glory of the soul-pursuing God.

Moses could have only dreamed of such a life.

LEARNING THE LANGUAGE OF DESIRE

So what does this mean for our experience of God? And what does it say about the quenching of our thirst? We get a hint of it in Romans 8:26–27:

> In the same way, the Spirit helps us in our weakness. We do not know what we ought to pray for, but the Spirit himself intercedes for us through wordless groans. And he who searches our hearts knows the mind of the Spirit, because the Spirit intercedes for God's people in accordance with the will of God.

This is a beautiful exploration of the Conversation and speaks to the primary way we experience God in our Dark Ocean: wordlessness. In this verse, Paul encourages us to look for God not in the external, nor in the voice of the mind so much as internal movements, what he calls "groans."

Groans are the language of love and desire. Groans are passionate, they speak much more than words because they're not limited to language. They're also not limited to our consciousness, nor our intellect. Whilst you and I go about our lives, the Spirit searches our hearts, He uncovers our longings and hopes and takes them to God.

God is always praying for you, in you, and through you. This is a communion of grace from beginning to end. Whilst you go about your living, God is listening to the unlanguaged thirsts within you, and He's responding. Prayer, then, as much as anything else, is about awakening to what Love feels and wants, and allowing our souls to soak it up like a sponge. That requires us learning to know, and live from, our Dark Ocean.

It requires, too, our consent.

Because by tuning in and saying *yes*, we become partners with Him in the life within us. We sink deeper in.

The degree to which we say *yes* will be the degree to which we experience and know Him, something we'll explore more later on. It's also the degree to which we'll see a transformed world around us. Because it's from this place, this Conversation, that we're also able to intercede more deeply for the world. Sharing God's thirst not only for ourselves, but others.

We tap into these groans by paying attention to the godly desires making their way up within us. When we grieve over injustice, we're experiencing the Conversation and may even be being invited to work amidst it in some way. When we feel a longing for others to know Jesus and His kingdom, we're hearing the invitation of the Spirit to do something about it. When songs want to make their way out, when we see ways to improve systems, educate children better, or develop an ache to see the church flourish, what we're hearing are the groans of the Spirit in wordless prayer, inviting us to participate in God, maybe even calling us to a vocation.

Often, when someone says they "hear God," it's these groans they're referring to. Not so much words or a mental conversation, but an inner knowing that comes from tuning in to the subtle movements of the Spirit within them. Learning to pay attention to the Conversation within me has been one of the main ways that I've discerned God's leading in my life. But it's also these groans, expressed in spiritual longing and a desire to know God more, that I've recognized to be His loving and wanting me too.

My very ache for God being God's ache for me.

For the longest time I couldn't not sing. Singing for me wasn't just about doing any old thing, it was vital to my soul. When I sang, I became myself, and in becoming myself, I felt a deep sense of God's presence. By "becoming myself," I mean that I felt most in tune with who I was at the very core of me and why I was alive when I sang. When I would sing, all anxiety, fear, and depression would evaporate and a deep stillness and peace would come over me. I would feel not like a musician in those moments, but an instrument. Made by God to be His song on earth.

It may sound a touch hyperbolic, but it's true.

For decades I would be doing something in the rhythm of my day when I would feel this deep pull, a tug on my heart that something wanted to come out. I'd pick up my guitar and, without thinking, open my mouth and sing. What came out was as much a gift and surprise to me as to those who may later hear it. It would reveal me to me, it would reveal what was happening deep down where I wasn't conscious.

It would articulate the groans of God within.

That same experience is true of prayer too. Prayer is a living gently aware of the movements of the Spirit within my Dark Ocean, and when they swell up, to do my best to lean in and flow with it. It may be a sudden longing for prayer or a sense of joy or love. It could be a particular grif, concern, or thought for a person. Whatever it is, it's an invitation to share God's desire and to experience Him more deeply within it.

That's what it means to be in the Conversation.

There is a grand space within us, made for God to fill with His loving, moving presence. That's not just a quaint statement about God's love filling us, but dynamic reality. We have been welcomed into the Conversation, the yearning of God for God, and for us.

We are caught up in Life.

That's not just some theological reality meant to tickle our intellectual and theological minds. It's something experiential, it's a new face-to-faceness, a vulnerability and friendship, a learning to live soul-nakedly with God. A drinking one another in.

It's an intimacy lived out not so much through external signs and wonders, but through the accessing of God's own heart through the groan of His longings. We're invited to listen to and be transformed by the life of God within us. Each time we pray, we should begin by breathing deeply and awakening to God's presence within us. With practice, returning to this *in*ness will lead to a continued presence of God and the meeting of our deepest thirst.

But this turning inward, to where God lives, comes with its challenges. We need to grow in our discerning the ebbs and flows, the different voices and rhythms of disorder within us that confuse our sense of Him. Awakening to our Dark Ocean and the groans within us is one thing, learning to navigate those undercurrents is another altogether.

Chapter 6

Discerning Movements

"May my mind remember
what my soul knows well—
that I am homed in
heavenly places."
Prayer Vol. 03

The groans of God aren't the only movements in our Dark Ocean. We are, all of us, a mix of confusing wants and impulses. Our fall into sin has messed with our compass. The harm of this world making its way into our very selves, our patterns of thinking and feeling.

All this disorder can become a fog on our spiritual lenses, obscuring our experience of God. If we don't learn to name it and discern between the voice of disorder and the voice of divine, thirsting love, we may find ourselves drinking from the wrong well.

This battle of voices takes place primarily in our minds where our aches, impulses, and disorder become thoughts and eventually actions. Only once our longings find expression in our thinking, and we ruminate on what to do with them, do they turn into something ordered or disordered, holy or unholy. In that way, our minds are powerful tools for turning toward or away from belovedness with the desires living within us.

If the purpose of desire is to draw us into a spousal, loving union with God through life in His Spirit, then retraining our minds, and in turn our thirsts, to abide in that reality is crucial. In fact, it's often in our unchecked, untamed thoughts that we are keeping ourselves from an awareness of God's yearning presence.

In our first year of marriage Katie experienced a similar form of chronic illness to what I have since. It started off occasional, but over the course of a year, she was laid out on the couch most nights in debilitating pain. Eventually, it caused her to give up her job. Doctors couldn't diagnose her illness and no treatments were working, we were getting desperate.

Then, one week a work colleague invited us to visit her church. My colleague's father was the pastor there and had a gift for seeing. Maybe, she suggested, he could help us figure out what was going on with Katie's health. So we went, a little unsure, but praying desperately for some kind of breakthrough. Straight after the gathering, whilst people were drinking coffee and beginning to plan their Sunday lunch, we were introduced. Immediately, without any small talk or offers for prayer, he started to prophesy.

As we stood there in a mixture of reverence and disbelief he described in amazing detail Katie's upbringing, her thoughts, and her struggles. It was as if he'd read her biography and was summarising her entire life. We were stunned, we'd never experienced anything like it. Katie said it was as if light had entered the darkness of her being.

She felt instantly healed. On the way home we took the drive-thru at Wendy's for a cheeseburger and, for the first time in years, ate it without any pain. It's been fifteen years since that Sunday morning and, praise God, it's never returned.

This pastor sent us off with only one invitation, to take every lie that Katie believed about how I felt about her, write it on a piece of paper, and allow me to speak the truth of my love in response. Part of the insight was that Katie had been carrying around these disbeliefs in her that didn't equate with reality. Disbeliefs about her acceptedness that were eating up her soul and, in turn, her body.

I loved her deeply and expressed it all the time, but the patterns of her mind kept her from a true experience of it. Her mind wasn't aligned with reality, and so despite the presence of my love daily, she rarely felt it in such a way she could deeply believe it.

This can happen to all of us. We can grow up in families where words were used as weapons, consciously or unconsciously, subtly or not, by those we love. Those words, once obvious and detectable when we're younger, hardwire themselves into the fabric of our thinking. Eventually, they became our mental operating system and we project them onto God too.

And so, we did what he suggested. We wrote every lie she believed and I spent time declaring the truth specifically over each one. Then, we took all those written lies and put them in a box under the bed, resolving that every time she had one of those thoughts, she would remind herself that they don't belong in her mind, but in the box under the bed.

This simple exercise transformed us, and it was an important part of Katie's physical healing.

All of us, in a similar way, for one reason or another, need the realignment of our minds with Reality. Because we all experience things that make us insecure, self-protecting, and afraid. Experiences that we then project onto God that rob us of seeing just how loved and full of Him we are.

We all need to learn to take our old ways of thinking and destructive mental patterns and turn away from them to His loving light. So that over time, as we retrain our thoughts, marrying them to Reality, we grow in a continual awareness and acceptance of the presence of God. Through our thoughts we can align our inner thirst for love with Truth.

Our pre-marriage counsellor once used the image of each person carrying their past relational experiences like luggage into their marriages. If we don't open it up and inspect it, we may end up wearing the clothes of our past hurts and expectations in the new world of our most important relationship. I love that image, it's perfect for what we bring to the table with God. If we don't inspect our old assumptions about ourselves, the world, and His nature, we'll project wrong ideas onto Him and wound communion.

Life in the Spirit is a life lived in opposition to these sinful patterns that are ingrained in our old selves. Patterns that warp the quenching of our deepest thirsts. It's not vague or up to chance, but practical, possible, and hopeful. But before we can explore how to live that way, we have to first make better sense of this disordered self we're learning to confront.

GOOD, BEAUTIFUL, TRUE

The Greek philosopher Plato famously used the three attributes of goodness, beauty, and truth as a way of describing the nature and reality of being. For him, capital R reality (whatever that was) had to hold a perfect harmony of these three things. Something couldn't be beautiful *and* evil and untrue, or good but ugly and false, etc.

This elegant philosophy became known to the world as the Transcendentals.

Later, Christian philosophers and theologians would offer their "amen" to this framework but with a crucial addition: the trinitarian God expressed and known in Christ is the divine expression of these three realities. Not so much because He *has* them, but because He *is* them. When we're talking about the divine yearning, about desire and the thirst that lives and breathes beneath our own, the Transcendentals can be a helpful beginning point for us in discerning between our ordered or disordered desire.

Because the language of desire, and following our desires, can lead us down some curly paths if we're not careful. Especially if we allow our thirst to be satisfied by what *feels good*, rather than what *is* good (i.e., truth). The former may temporarily satisfy but will ultimately lead to deeper disorder and ache. It's only in the good *and* true that we will find ultimate fulfilment.

We live in a world that calls desire good but has unhinged it from the True. We despise external rules and accountabilities and preach a moral relativism, a "do what works for you" approach that essentially equates feelings with truth. We may dabble in some neuroscience or the odd Eastern spiritual practice, but even with those we'll likely have an "if it doesn't fit me I won't do it" mentality.

That may sound like liberation, but it results in a terrifying, albeit often unarticulated, disorientation. Living at the whims of our thirsts makes us not a victor but a slave, because it assumes that we know *why* we want what we want, let alone that we have any control over wanting it. But what if what we want is the result of our woundedness, our culture, or our misunderstandings about how the world works?

If you've spent any length of time acting on your impulses rather than interrogating them, you'll know how exhausting, disappointing, and discouraging it can be and how often we change our minds. We need salvation from our thirsts, a goodness outside ourselves that is also true. A way out of our malfunctioning operating system.

If our longings spring from our disorder then we need a control, something to hold them up against to see the wood for the trees. That's impossible with a moral relativism that bases truth on subjective personal experience. We need something else.

WE'RE NOT WHO WE WERE

As we've seen, in the beginning this *dis*-ease of ours, imaged in God, was intended as a holy turbine that would drive us to God in love and vitality. Because God dignifies us, He gave us a choice as to what we'd do with this longing and the capacity to learn to fully give it over to Him.

Sadly, as we read in Genesis 1, we chose not to fulfil our ache in love, but turned it in on ourselves. In Christian theology we call this "the fall." What's most important about this fall isn't so much that it resulted in people who make mistakes (although that's also true) as our taking on a disposition of disorderedness. Or what we call a fallen nature.

We could say that our fallen nature is our default misuse of the divine gift of desire, turning it toward ourselves and the world instead of divine communion. Scripture describes it as our "old self" or our "sinful nature,"[53] depending on the translation, but in the New Testament it is most commonly translated as the "flesh."

Our fallen nature is our proclivity and magnetism toward a disordered self. That original fall has worked its way so definitively into the human condition that all our mental, emotional, and spiritual frames of seeing the world are shaped by it. We're so disordered, in other words, that we think it's normal.

The flesh is our *eros* gone rogue, living without *agape*.

The New Testament word for "flesh" is usually translated directly from the Greek word *sarx*. *Sarx*, importantly, refers to what's fallen about us, not what's physical. It's our sarx that prefers to use sex as a means to get what we want, rather than give of ourselves to one person in love. It's our sarx that wants to take up power that we might control others and be elevated in society, rather than use it to empower and uplift others. Our sarx wants to take things rather than earn them, to use, abuse, and destroy. In the divine marriage, it's our sarx that wants to continue on as we did when we were single, getting the "best" of both worlds.

It's important to differentiate between our sarx as our disorder and our actual physical body. Because sex, eating, earning money, and everything else we do in this world is a gift from God. Seeing those things as evil leads into all sorts of new problems. They only become disordered when we use them as an end in and of themselves, like expecting sex to satisfy our deepest longing for connection and being seen, or for food and drink to fill the void of boredom and spiritual hunger we feel, etc.

The New Testament writers treat the physical body as neutral, it can be used for good or evil ends depending on the nature (our fallen nature or the Holy Spirit which is God's nature) we submit it to.

There are two dangers in confusing our flesh (sarx) with our bodies (soma). The first we've already explored a little and that is our seeing bodily things as either lesser than, or outright unholy or unimportant. This dualism affects our everyday lives when the things that are natural to us, that we must do, like clean, administrate, and work, feel at odds with the kingdom of heaven. If we believe this, prayer and experiencing God are relegated to the little time we have to offer when we're not doing the "other" stuff.

Spirituality becomes, then, unearthed and antithetical to the very life God made us for.

But if being in a body is a problem, then someone needs to tell Jesus. Because He had to eat, drink, clean the dishes, pay His bills, and do the rest of it just like we do, and He did it all in perfect, unbroken, and sinless communion with His Father. Our bodies aren't the issue then, what we're letting guide them is.

The second danger is that we equate our sarx thirsts, our fallen and "fleshly" ones, with the truth and goodness of a holy thirst. And by that I mean we come to believe that our fallen nature, our disordered eros, is good. The modern version of this is a "my truthism" that assumes if something is at odds with what makes me happy, or makes me feel good, then it can't be the right thing.

If we mistake our sarx thirsts for godly ones, we lose our palette for truth. Part of our life in the Spirit is our learning to partner with God in recalibrating our spiritual taste-buds for true goodness.

In the most intense years of my chronic health journey, I went on a highly restrictive fast in the hope of healing my immune system. It was intense. For a whole year I gave up gluten, dairy, yeast, carbo-hydrates, legumes, root vegetables, starches, sugars of any kind (including fruits), alcohol, and coffee. Although, I have to confess, I couldn't completely give up the coffee!

The problem is, I grew up in a family that appreciated a treat. When my parents put on a meal for us, we would have to roll out of our dining chairs afterward. My parents were incredible hosts, they loved spending time with people and making them feel at home. One of the ways they did that was through good food.

But we were also prone to the sweet stuff. Some of my favourite memories as a family were staying up late with a block of dark forest chocolate or Memphis Meltdown ice creams, talking about life, faith, and the wonder of God. There were always treats in our home, they were part of family life.

By the time I was in my twenties, I'd continued the worst of those habits. A coke and a milky bar for 3:30-itis (that impossible mid-afternoon energy slump) and another for dessert before bed. I didn't think anything of it. I thought everyone ate that way. I've got much better after a big turnaround seven years ago, but it's remained one of the old luggage items I've had to deal with.

Suffice to say, taking on this new restrictive diet like this was a big deal.

And I hated it.

Every day of the first few months was painful. I was hungry all the time, felt low on energy, and morbidly sorry for myself whenever we had dinner with friends. I started shortly before Christmas and summer (we have both at the same time here in the Southern Hemisphere), so you can imagine how often I was reminded of what I couldn't have.

But around eight weeks in, something began to shift. I stopped craving sugars and carbs altogether. In fact, when someone ate an ice cream or popped a fizzy drink around me, the intense sweet smell put me off. Eventually, something even weirder happened. At the end of it all, when I was able to eat some of those foods again, I didn't even really enjoy them. Alcohol made me feel foggy and sugar and carbs taxed my newfound consistent energy.

My desires had been realigned.

I thought it was the food that I wanted. I thought it was the food that made me happy. But it was actually the *idea* of it, the fantasy that it did something which in reality it didn't, that was motivating me. As it turned out, what I thought was good—carbs, sugars, treats, and eating whatever I wanted—actually made me feel bad. When I went off it, I started to crave salads for the first time in my life, prefer vegetarian meals, and to generally eat and drink less out of want rather than duty.

That's exactly what we must learn to do with our disordered desires.

The more we turn away from feelings of shame, condemnation, self-hate, anxiety, lust, unforgiveness, and anger, the more we begin to love the good thoughts of peace, presence, and love. We reset our spiritual palettes, our ways of being, and make room for God. This begins with reading and knowing the truth of God's teaching in Scripture and its outworking in Christian community, but for it to transform us it needs to move from our heads to our hearts. It needs to be experienced in prayer.

By not feeding thoughts that lead our thirst toward disorder we starve off our cravings for what is harmful, and calibrate our palette for holiness and the presence of God. We learn to despise our disorder and love the good, beautiful, and true.

Seventeenth-century Carmelite Brother Lawrence, in his profound book *Practicing the Presence of God*, put it beautifully:

> I make it my business only to persevere in his holy presence, wherein I keep myself by a simple attention, and a general fond regard to God, which I may call an *actual presence of God*; or to speak better, an habitual, silent, and secret conversation of the soul with God.[54]

For Brother Lawrence, the presence of God is a continual awareness of Him, a setting upon His love with one's thoughts. To do that we have to clear our minds of obsessive and destructive thought habits that interrupt to draw us away from Reality.

As the wisdom goes, "Beware thoughts, for they become words. Beware words, for they become our actions. Beware actions, for they become our habits. Beware habits, for they become our character."[55] Thoughts, in other words, are the seeds of life. What we allow in ours becomes us.

We don't overcome our minds by fighting our negative thoughts but by turning back toward the loving presence of God whenever they arrive. What we're talking about is the reorienting of our desires through the union of our minds with the Spirit who abides within us. To build this spiritual muscle in our lives I'd like to suggest two practices.

MEDITATING ON GOD'S THIRST

The first practice I have for checking my disordered thirsts seems, initially, like it's not connected. It's the practice of experiencing God's good and right thirst for me, and in me, every day. By that I mean taking time every morning to set my attention on the pursuing, loving, and present God who dwells within.

If you've ever seen a barbershop quartet sing live, you may have noticed one of them using a mouth instrument to play a single note before the group started singing. This one note hones each of the four singers into a single key to sing in. It's their unifying principle, all their melody and harmony is built in the key this one single starting note offers. That's what a morning routine of tuning in to the voice of love within us does for our experience of God's presence in our thirsts. It reminds them of their reference point, their Good End. By experiencing the Transcendental, we create a control to discern Him in the movements of our deep self throughout our day.

The way I practise this is by beginning with calming my body down with slow, deep breathing. Slowing our bodies down helps land us in the present, where God lives. So often, especially with the ubiquity of devices, our nervous systems are on hyperdrive. God is slow, quiet, still. We need to slow down to meet Him.

Next, whilst allowing my thoughts to be what they'll be, I imagine myself sinking deeper down into my Dark Ocean. For me, I visualise that movement being from my head down into my stomach, where I imagine my soul is homed.

As I sit there, experiencing God's presence soaking me through, I look to Him. I tune in to the quiet groans of His Spirit, allowing

Him to speak through them. By "speak through them," I don't mean with words or information. What I'm looking for is an alignment of *being*, of union, of our becoming-oneness. This kind of prayer is a communion of thirsts, God's longing for me intermingling with mine for Him.

If pictureless prayer is difficult, I might imagine Jesus on the cross as an expression of His profound, thirsting love. I might meditate on Jesus' words "As the Father has loved me so have I loved you" and allow that reality to permeate my being. The key is to align our longing with God's consciously in prayer, through His presence. As we do that, we create a reference point to return to later in the day when we want to turn back to God and live in conscious union with His presence.

Practising this communion every day, over time, resets my internal operating systems. It sets me right and creates a control for my spirit for the rest of the day by creating a True North for my desires and a reference for a clear mind set on Him.

In time, it helps me begin to better and more quickly see when I'm deviating from setting my desires on God, living out of disorder. It's a loving prevention, a longer, slower journey of bringing my being into God's rightness.

CLOTHING OURSELVES IN CHRIST

The second practice I have for bringing my desire into alignment with God's for the reordering of my heart is what Saint Paul calls "clothing ourselves" with Christ. In Romans 13:14 he says, "Rather, clothe yourselves with the Lord Jesus Christ, and do not think about how to gratify the desires of the flesh."

There's a beautiful simplicity here. Paul doesn't ask us to wrestle with our disordered desires head-on, but to simply turn our thoughts away from them back toward Christ. In other words, to not let our minds run off with ruminations about how to act on our disordered reflexes but to starve them off at their root.

Think of how quickly a little anger can turn into a vitriolic, self-justifying inner monologue with the person who upset you. They don't even know you're angry before you had the entire fight with them in your mind all day long! Or feelings of sexual longing that turn into an obsessive state of mind, eventually leading to a plot to do something unhealthy about it.

It's not easy to shut these kinds of thoughts down right at their genesis. In fact, at the start it's jarring. The longer we've held lies and patterns of giving in to our thoughts, the harder it will be. But by turning away from gratifying these thoughts and desires when they come, we slowly domesticate them and, through the Spirit, are transformed.

Our powerful feelings and desires are convincing and want us to believe that there's no way to resist them. They'll tell us we've always given in, that this is all we'll ever be, that we don't have the strength to say no to them now. The world says the same, hoping we'll give up on turning from disorder so they can continue to sell us their products and ideologies as the solution.

But that's not biblical Christianity. The gospel is the promise that not only is transformation possible, it's the very business of God. God doesn't leave us to the powerful desires of the flesh, he gives us His Spirit, beckoning us to partner with Him in our liberation.

What Paul suggests is a simple turning away from the disordered thoughts within us that draw us *from* God, and a turning *toward* God Himself. We don't fight the thoughts, we don't try to think nothing, we instead fill ourselves with an awareness of God's presence. I love the image of clothing ourselves in Christ, as if we're simply taking off the old, ragged garment of disorder and putting on the new, clean clothes of joyful love.

And notice how Paul uses the language of desires.

This is a *choosing* of which thirst we give in to.

The way we practise this is by every time a powerful desire springs up, and we're tempted to use fallen means to satisfy it, running toward an awareness of God's presence instead. I do this by simply saying in my mind or out loud, "No, I choose to clothe myself with Christ" or "This isn't what I want, Beloved, I want You."

I imagine my Dark Ocean opening up to God, allowing Him to fill that space instead. I give Him the chance to be enough.

I might also remind myself of a truth opposite to the lie I'm being told. If I'm angry, rather than internalising self-righteous arguments, I turn myself instead toward Christ's forgiving statement over His enemies on the cross. If I feel low, I remember Psalm 21, that God is with me in my valleys of death and sorrow. If it's lust, God's invitation to love. Anxiety, His unceasing calm and rest.

At first, it may take some time to notice our runaway thoughts. We're well used to disorder, remember. But as we consciously spend time in prayer each morning, and practise clothing ourselves in God's presence whenever we *do* notice we're off track, we'll slowly cut off the thirsts at the root and experience transformation. True, God-led, and love-inspired transformation.

The union of our consciousness with God.

This isn't about fighting our thirsts, but about using them as triggers to bring us into an awareness and experience of God's presence. To clothe our minds in belovedness. However powerful your disordered thirst may be, and I know how powerful and consuming they are at times, through this practice and God's loving grace you'll overcome it and more fully enter the union of God in your inner being.

We're imaged after a God of desire, but this yearning beneath our yearning is often obscured by the chaos of our disorder. A fallen nature that takes time to articulate, let alone seek God amidst.

Because of sin, and because of the misappropriation of our love by this world, we can't just always trust good feelings as being the presence of God, or even guiding us to Him. We have to discern the movements within us, allowing Love to forever draw us toward what is good, beautiful, and true, and not to that which sells us short of belovedness.

The deepest road to healing, to the collecting up of ourselves again into oneness with God, is our sitting *in* Him in our Dark Ocean. It's our daily experiencing Him right at the base of us where our thirst is most potent, allowing Him to transform us into His image. Communion like this isn't only intimate and life-giving, but it's the key to reordering our bent thirsts and collecting us back into wholeness.

Communion, however, isn't only a mind thing. It's an all-of-our-living kind. So to bring our souls into the bright-lit reality of God's invitation to love, we turn now to bringing our bodies into harmony with this new intermingling life.

Chapter 7

Fidelity

"Sow in me, in the soil of my heart,
Your word, Your vision, the way
You long to get things done, that in
my being like You, we may be one."

Prayer Vol. 04

On tour in the US one summer I met a gifted musician obsessed with making it big. Every time we talked I left inspired to dream bigger myself, they just had that kind of energy to them.

But as I got to know them better, I noticed that their lifestyle didn't seem to match their passion. They hardly practised, didn't take any shows that weren't a big enough deal, never risked their finances, and weren't willing to do the difficult work of finishing songs. All things that are crucial aspects of the journey in becoming what they were hoping to become. In their mind, they were a passionate, committed musician. In reality, they were doing nothing about it.

Their life was lived contrary to their identity.

I don't judge them either, in fact, I can sympathise. Whether it's StrengthsFinder, Enneagram, Genius, or some other personality or gift test, I always come up embarrassingly mind heavy. I think *a lot* and spend a lot of time reading books and entering prayerful space. It's easy to read the monastics, very difficult to live like one. It's also very easy to love goodness, beauty, and truth and not actually appropriate it in my life. Especially when, like me, it's so intellectually satisfying in the first place.

This is part of the gift of who God made me, but the danger is that I can equate my internal life, my desire to follow God and engage with the world, with the actual work of doing it. I have to work hard to not only love the teaching of goodness, but to live it.

Union with God is the same.

Consider our image of marriage. Yes it's an emotional, mental, romantic commitment, but if all that internalised beauty doesn't make its way out of us into our living, it becomes meaningless. Marriage is about living *life* together, not just emotional connection. The great commandment, remember, is to love God with all our hearts, minds, and strength.[56] There we find the key to satisfying our thirst in our everyday living.

A life of holy fidelity.

It's important to think of holy fidelity, or what we usually speak of as obedience, as the outworking of our belovedness, and not as our way of earning it. We seek to live as Jesus teaches us, not to earn God's love or to please Him, but to stay true to Him and even to ourselves. Though it doesn't always feel like it, obedience actually makes us more us.

Because as we enter an intermingling life with God, *He* becomes our identity. Living in opposition to our new selves, then, our Christ selves, jars our spirit and makes us feel as if we're out of kilter with ourselves.

It's here that God's desire to marry us begins to offer something essential to our day-to-day living. Where it moves from being a quaint metaphor for a minority of mystics to becoming a liberating framework for every one of us in the decisions we make each moment.

Because marriage is the living out of what's already true. It's where emotional love gives birth to an experiential one. The more a couple is able to live toward each other, the more mentally, spiritually, and emotionally integrated they become, the more wholistically satisfying their love is. Could there be a better image for divine communion?

The satisfying of our spiritual thirst comes with our learning to integrate our whole selves with God in this new divine marriage. Through fidelity to Jesus' teaching, we have an actual experience of God's goodness, purity, and other-love. Of His presence.

As a teen, I loved God deeply in my heart, but as I shared earlier, I had a proclivity for living in the opposite direction. By that I mean I had a strong, emotional, and mental connection to God but a poorly *lived* one. I didn't so much practise Jesus' teachings of chastity, humility, prayer, and generosity, for example, as much as admire them. In practice, it all felt restrictive to me. Wasn't God, after all, only after my heart?

I'd been sold on a "personal relationship" with God based on conversation alone. Intentions mattered most, and poor behaviour could always be forgiven. I had no paradigm for experiencing Jesus' teachings as the very invitation to a deeper experience of God that they truly are. I hadn't learned to love goodness yet.

For me, Jesus' commandments were an impossible standard to keep and attempting to do so was "religious" and "lifeless." I didn't at all *love* them. I found myself instead riding mountain-top experiences through to low valleys of shame and guilt. Knowing God, for me, was an existential rollercoaster.

But after my experience that New Year's where God called Katie and me home, all that changed. I had a supercharged desire to drink God deeply, and the more I fed it, the greater it grew. I began to feel like I would do anything to live the kind of life I'd read saints before me had discovered. To experience God more for myself.

I would scour Jesus' teachings in the Gospels and find ways to immediately obey them. I forgave those who hurt me, and asked their forgiveness in return. I gave as much of my money away as I could, tangibly loved those in my life, and told almost everyone I met the gospel and offered to pray for them. It's also then that I learned the true power of prayer and what Jesus meant when He taught, "Knock and the door will be opened to you."[57]

I took the third year off my university degree to wake at 5:00 each morning and spend three hours or so in the Scriptures and prayer. I would pray through each verse, asking the Spirit to sear it to my heart, loving every word as a vehicle for helping me know and experience God more deeply. I wouldn't move on from any line until I'd reckoned personally with it and sought a way to respond tangibly that day.

I took my Bible with me everywhere. I took it to the doctor's to read whilst in the waiting room, to cafés whilst I waited for coffee. On any break I would steal myself away to read and pray. None of it was burdensome, none of it felt religious. I just wanted to be as close to Him as I could humanly be. My newfound faith carried a distinct living intensity.

There was one major difference between this new fervour and the longing of my teen years, one defining feature that came to mark this renewal I was experiencing. I actually *wanted* to live a fierce fidelity. What changed? Why did the very thing that kept me from God only years before now become the very centre of my faith?

It was my encounter with the thirst of God. When God spoke to me in my mess, and I experienced His astounding acceptance and love of me, I wanted to return it. Not out of duty, but out of desire.

Now I experienced Jesus' teaching no longer as a set of rules I had to obey to please God but the very keys to drinking Him in to my soul's fill. In God's invitation to fidelity I no longer saw an expectation to meet to please Him, but the shape of a life that already has Him. And the more I lived this teaching I'd marginalised, the less anxious, more joyful, more patient and loving I became. The power that the New Testament so regular speaks of became an experienced reality in my life.

With the grace and help of the Spirit, I was becoming like God, learning to love what He loves, aligning my living with His nature, and in so doing, experiencing Him more.

That learning to live Jesus' teachings brings us into harmony with love, vitality, and union with God should make it something we pine for with the same voracity as life itself, but so few of us feel that way. Why is that? Why are we so unmotivated toward actually doing the good Jesus teaches us instead of just admiring and talking about it?

For me, I see two significant and interconnected reasons. The first is that living Jesus' teaching is difficult and profoundly costly. Maybe we can forgive someone who offends or hurts us once or twice, but seventy-seven times?[58] What about deep and persistent feelings of anger, lust, or jealousy that don't go away easily, if ever? The kind that ruminate and return no matter how hard we try to overcome them. Or trusting God's provision so decisively that we're never anxious for work or money and freely give our lives away in radical generosity?

We all love the ideals of these things, but living them takes a huge amount of grit, persistence, and a willingness to give up on what feels good in the moment. The truth is, we thirst to be those kinds of people, to be free of our lust, greed, jealousy, and anger, but the road to becoming them requires harder work in the interim than we often feel we have the strength for.

That's why it must begin with an experience of God's thirst for us and an energising of *His* Spirit. We cannot stir up that kind of zeal and strength on our own. Living in fidelity begins not with our love, but God's. John the apostle tells us, remember, that "we love because he first loved us."[59] Fidelity is our *yes* to that love.

Secondly, without a paradigm shift on what God's commandments are meant to be for us, we can slip into the other reason I believe many of us do not live our lives in harmony with God's. That is, we see obedience as a bar we need to reach to please God and earn His love and presence, rather than as the very map for liberation our deeper selves desire. Fear, guilt, and shame are terrible motivators. There will be no transformation in our spiritual lives if they're centred on pleasing and earning love. Only Love can motivate love.

God's commandments are His love letter to us, His vows. To help you see that, I want to turn to the one place many people see the opposite. The giving of the law on Mount Sinai and the Ten Commandments.

THE COMMANDMENTS, GOD'S LOVE LETTER

We've already explored the way in which Scripture, since the beginning, has told the story of God as Husband to humanity and His desire to ultimately make good on His promise to be one. Yet the Old Testament doesn't always read like the romance stories we're used to. Partly because it's a large, disorienting, ancient book. But partly too because we've been taught to read it a certain way, transactionally.

There's one vital place we can return to, to rethink what fidelity is and what God's commandments mean to us. What I love about this particular story is that many of us read it not as a place of God's spousal love, but as a demonstration, instead, of His terror. A place to go to learn how to *please* God rather than soak in His affectionate and profound eros-agape love. Because of that, it's the perfect place to go to rediscover what fidelity really is. On Mount Sinai, woven into the narrative of Israel's birth as a nation, we find the language not of fear, wrath, and performance, but of a marriage proposal. What in a traditional Hebrew marriage is called a *ketubah*.

The ketubah is a marriage contract, offered by a husband to the wife as a promise of care, protection, love, and commitment for the rest of their lives. It included the practicalities of how a husband would look after his lover and protect her from any potential violation of her rights, making it harder for a man to divorce her in a time when women had little protection.

A ketubah is not a dowry or a purchase, but an agreement that the married couple would both share to live a fruitful, loving marriage. On the journey toward union, a Hebrew woman would commonly hear and expect five important words from her romantic other: *lakah*, *segullah*, *mikveh*, *ketubah*, and *huppah*. Each a sign of the love and commitment on the path toward marriage.

As it turns out, all of these are found in God's language toward Israel in Exodus and in the very giving of the Ten Commandments. Beginning with lakah.

In the book of Exodus, Israel is still in Egypt, in captivity by an oppressive pharaoh. Through Moses, God speaks to the Hebrew people declaring Himself to be their God and reveals His intention to save them by bringing them out of Egypt. In Exodus 6:6–7, we find God saying, "I will free you from being slaves to them, and I will redeem you with an outstretched arm and with mighty acts of judgement. *I will take you as my own people, and I will be your God.*" That entire final line in the original Hebrew could be summarised in the word *lakah.*

When a man said lakah to a woman, it was a declaration of romantic intent, it was to say, "I want to make you my own." Lakah takes a relationship out of the friend zone and into exclusivity. It's a declaration of desire. When Israel hears this, their ears perk up. Is this God of Moses really going to propose to us? They may have begun anticipating what would come next. How serious is God here?

They are waiting to see if God would say, "Segullah."

Segullah means "treasured possession" and is more than just a commitment, it's a declaration of affection and beautification, and in Exodus 19:5 we hear God declare to them, "Now if you obey me fully and keep my covenant, then out of all nations you will be my *treasured possession.*"

In segullah, God affirms His desire not only to be Israel's God and King, but her husband too. God doesn't only want Israel, He wants to beautify her, shower her with affections, set her apart as His own, treasure her with all of His being. This must have been an astounding realisation for the Hebrew people to have. They're discovering that God doesn't only want to free them from slavery, but that He longs for something far more personal.

To add to the drama, they're about to hear Him say *mikvah.*

Mikvah is less affection oriented and more practical and essential. It means "to go and wash oneself, to be consecrated," and in the ancient Near East in particular it would occur through a three-day ceremonial washing. This made the bride ritually pure and ready for the wedding day.

The mikvah comes in Exodus 19:10–11 when God says to Moses, "Go to the people and consecrate them today and tomorrow. Make them wash their clothes and be ready by the third day, because on that day the LORD will come down on Mount Sinai in the sight of all the people."

Now Israel is sure they're about to experience something magnificent. A nation-founding moment. Their invitation to mikvah is a clear call to prepare for a profound encounter with their new Spouse. That something is their *ketubah*, the commandments of Mount Sinai.

Scholars have described the Ten Commandments as God's wedding vows to humanity. His way of saying, "This is how I love you, will you love Me this way back?" That doesn't mean they didn't become the somewhat ethical and legal basis of the nation of Israel, just that they arrived couched in the shape of a Husband wanting to be one with the object of His affection. His marriage proposal.

The first commandment to "have no other gods before me" is much like the vow we make today when we say, "I take *you* to be my lawfully wedded wife/husband." It's our declaration to choose one over every other. An offering of loving fidelity. God has already declared His undying love for us, the first commandment is our simply returning that same affection.

The second is similar, the call to make no image of another god is our promise to not settle for lesser things. To not be distracted by the gifts of God, what He's made and His provision, turning toward them instead of His person. It's the promise to not belittle Him but to allow Him to be who He is—mystery, wonder, *other*. In our not making another image, we preserve His uniqueness in our relationship.

The third, not to misuse His name, is commonly misunderstood. It doesn't mean not using His name as a swear word, although that's also dishonouring. It's about the way we live as His wife. When we marry, we're no longer only an individual, we become part of each other. This is often exemplified in the woman taking on the husband's last name either exclusively or as well as her own in Western cultures.

If one does something harmful to another or to the world, then both are implicated, because it comes now not only from the offender but also their new family unit. From their shared name. Their oneness brings a powerful accountability to their love. To take on someone's name is to take *them* on, and when it dishonours them by living in opposition to the relationship and who they are, it harms the relationship.

We could go on, but you can see how understanding marriage as the context for the commandments begins to transform them from a list of "dos and don'ts" to an invitation to experience the vitality of divine love through the way we live. We can see they're not an invitation to obey in order to please and be accepted, but as a way of enjoying the pleasure and acceptance we already have.

After the man had offered his ketubah and the bride had accepted, he would go and prepare the wedding celebration. When he returned, the two would experience the final step in the ketubah, the *huppah*.

Huppah means "under the presence." There were two kinds, the first was the marriage altar which the bride and groom stood underneath. The second was in the marriage chamber where a prayer shawl would be fastened above the bed to represent the presence of God over the marriage as it was consummated.

In the Exodus story we find the huppah in chapter 20 verse 18, where we read, "Now all the people witnessed the thunderings, the lightning flashes, the sound of the trumpet, and the mountain smoking; and when the people saw it, they trembled and stood afar off."[60] What was the canopy that Israel saw? The very presence of God descending on Mount Sinai itself. A great cloud full of lightnings and thunderings.

A ketubah.

The word used for "lightnings" here isn't lighting in the way that you and I understand it, but is a glorified fire. It's actually the same word used for Moses' burning-bush experience. Likewise "thundering" is the Hebrew word *kole*, which in most other places in Scripture is translated as "voices" or "languages." It could be read as "The people witnessed flames of fire and voices."

Because of this, Hebrew commentators suggest that what Israel heard from the mountain that day was God saying, "Will you marry Me?" In the rabbinical tradition it's even said that on this day God proposed to Israel in seventy thousand tongues of fire, a number representing every tribe and nation on earth. Each flaming tongue going out from the mountain and touching each Israelite on the head before returning to God.

Hundreds of years later, the Spirit would descend again in a whole new consummation on that very same day in what we know as the festival of Pentecost. Except this time those very same tongues of fire would *stay* upon the heads of God's people, and from within them would come languages announcing the new age of union.

A whole new divine intimacy was born.

SPIRIT-EMPOWERED FIDELITY

God is passionate about us, He created us for oneness. But in our disorder, our sin and brokenness, our hearts lead us toward all kinds of other loves and paths, even when we so desperately want to find ourselves in God. And so, to help us shape our love in such a way as it will always lead us back to Him, He teaches us how to live so that living the commandments of God expands our hearts, setting us toward His face, and satisfies our thirst.

They're a *positive* force.

If I live a life of fidelity out of my thirst for love, God's commandments will be liberating, personal, full of life, joy, and peace. If I do them out of duty and obligation, or even worse, fear, they will fruit anger, self-righteousness, shame, divine insecurity, or powerful self-hate.

It's in *desire* that our hearts come alive, not fear.

Jesus continues to frame fidelity as a response to love rather than our ability to earn it when He tells His disciples, "As the Father has loved me, so have I loved you. *Now remain in my love.*"[61] Notice the movement here. Jesus tells us that He loves us like God loves us. No prerequisite, no criteria, God's love is freely offered. God proposes and loves first.

Then, He invites us to *stay* in His love. That's what the commandments are, a map for abiding, not performing. They're an invitation to live from in the Spirit. When I stop, quieten down in the place of prayer, and receive God's thirsting love for me, I practise living *from* love rather than *for* it. I can start by praying, "Holy Spirit, show me Your love and help me live from it," then take the time to practise welcoming this love into my being through prayer. It's from this place of inner stillness and rested love that fidelity begins to become natural.

When I find myself feeling fidelity as a burden rather than a liberation, I can diagnose it as a lack of sitting in God's presence, receiving His thirst for me. Then, asking for the Spirit's help again, I return to the well of love to drink and be recalibrated. I could do this one hundred times in a day if I'm struggling to overcome a habit in my life or wrestling with temptation. By returning to God's presence instead of fighting it, I get the strength I need.

Fidelity is the work of the Spirit, beginning to end so that our living love is more about abiding than proving. Is about the strength of God's love, not our willpower. The only striving is to create a routine of prayerful return to God's love and to let that continually reorient us toward goodness, beauty, and truth. If we work hard to foster this prayerful living, the rest of our working will flow from love.

It's for that reason that some monastics saw prayer as warfare. Because *choosing* prayer when our bodies and minds are screaming to go in the opposite direction is a real discipline. When we do finally give ourselves to God's loving presence in the heat of battle, we rarely regret it. But overcoming those powerful forces in the moment, and choosing prayer even if we feel lukewarm and uninspired, is a kind of battle.

But so is giving in to a way of living that harms our dignity and draws us away from the Love we so desperately thirst for. We are all thirsty and need to drink, it will be either disorder or love. There's no third option. It may feel easier to give in to the power of disorder in the moment when the feelings are strong, but the grief of our disconnection with the experience of God's presence will be just as, if not more, grieving.

If we resist, though, and do warfare in our minds and bodies when our thirst wants to draw us from, and not move us toward, the union our deepest self longs for, the pain is acute in temptation, but the joy, intimacy, and communion that result are greater than anything we've given up. Either way, we do battle with our thirsts. Why not battle for goodness rather than disappointment?

Jesus invites us to *remain* in the love He's already unequivocally given. To simply not step out of it. That's key. Fidelity isn't about getting God's loving presence, it's about not walking away from it. To us, that feels like hard work because we're so used to living antithetical to love. But to God, it's our simply learning to live in the way of true freedom.

Remember the restrictive diet I went on to heal my immune system? A few months into it, I noticed something happening to my senses. When someone opened a banana across the room, the smell would overwhelm me. The sweetness of it was intoxicating. I could smell what people were cooking houses away, and any herbs or spices I put in any of my food permeated the taste more powerfully.

Honing in my diet focused my senses and I experienced food in a whole new intensity.

Before, I'd been consuming so much sugar and carbs that fruit and vegetables tasted far less desirable than packaged food. But as I gave up all the extra sweeteners I thought I wanted, natural, whole foods—the stuff God made—tasted so much sweeter. I stopped craving all the things we created to get the more we want out of food. It turned out I just couldn't taste the goodness of the world as it was because I was so used to a toxic diet.

My desires changed.

That's God's offer in the teachings of Jesus, or what we call His commands.

Even at times when it's hard, even when it feels contrary to the thirsts groaning within us, living Jesus' way sharpens our emotional, spiritual, and mental taste-buds to learn to love the Way we were created to live. To learn to love goodness.

And in doing so, we awaken.

God's commandments are a manual for reordering the disorder in our thirst. They give it a right shape. God's shape. They don't dampen our zeal, they unchain it. They don't take our freedom, they liberate it. Because in them we find the freedom to get what we *really* want beneath what we think we do.

Jesus tells us in John 14:6, "I am the way, the truth, and the life."[62] Fidelity, even in the face of our powerful thirsts to the contrary, is our believing Him when He says it.

NUMBNESS, A CURE

Have you ever felt a pervasive numbness in your prayer life? Like there's just no moving your heart, no ache, no desire? This ambivalence appears to us not so much in an attitude of all-out rebellion, but in a lack of motivation to know God more, or to desire more vitality in life in general. A *meh*ness toward prayer.

The monastics called it "acedia," or "the noonday demon." A lukewarmness that hits us like the boredom of a long midday. It can show up because we're wrestling with real-life struggles such as depressive attitudes and thoughts, chronic health, grief, or the traumas of life. But it's also a symptom of our feasting on the wrong diet.

Living in worldliness, as it turns out, is a sedative to our communion.

In Matthew 24:12 we find Jesus drawing an interesting parallel between love and fidelity. Speaking of the world of the future He says, "Sin will be rampant everywhere, and the love of many will grow cold."[63] Notice the correlation. Sin (our disorder, misapplied thirst, and willful living-away from Love) will be everywhere, and as a result the lamp of love will dim. Numbness is often the result of God-oppositional living.

We cannot live as we like, giving in to disorder and living without care and attention to the good and beautiful ways of Jesus, *and* have a vital spiritual life. Any area we don't give over to Love eventually sedates us. The more we refuse to bring our living into the shape of love, the higher the dose until we enter a spiritual sleep. God-oppositional living and numbness go hand in hand.

All intimacy, all union, depends on the security and safety of loving the One. Seeking to satisfy our thirst in worldliness grieves the heart of God and dishonours the sacred union between us. But it also has the effect of cooling our own love.

Astonishingly, though it grieves God, it doesn't change His unceasing love toward us. But for our part, we begin to feel more and more distant from Him. Our prayers become dry and cold, our desire for satisfying our souls in His presence diminishes, our vitality for life gets replaced with compulsions and addictions. Slowly, we lose the light of love.

Some years ago, after reading this very passage, I determined that whenever my prayer life began to wane or my heart was hardening, I would take stock of my life to see where I wasn't loving God with my living. Almost every time I would notice a correlation with watching too much TV, harbouring anger, being selfishly ambitious with work or jealous of others.

The more we consecrate our lives, the more we live a life of loving fidelity, the greater our love grows and the more natural it becomes to live that way. We cannot live how we want *and* be married to God. In living Jesus' teaching, we awaken to love, receive a vital spirit, experience His presence, and grow in union with our Beloved.

To say *yes* to God's proposal for soul-deep union with us, we need to offer more than just our theological sentiment or emotional goodwill. Our lives must follow. With the *yes* of our bodies to God's commands, alongside the consent of our minds to His truth and greater reality, we no longer live at odds with our own desire for Him.

We're finally collected back together in a loving unity of self.

When we live this way, our prayer and our living become one and the same. Communion engulfs all of life. Because we're not praying, asking for God's loving presence, and then living in a way that distorts love and, in turn, our own vision. Instead, we're experiencing God's love for us, *through* our love for others, the world, and ourselves, in a very trinitarian, "give away to receive" kind of life.

But there's much more to the story of our living union with God. Much of the grandest movements happen much deeper, in our allowing the Spirit to love and transform us. Ultimately, it's in our long-living, in our vulnerability, in our pain, and in our living fully seen and open toward Him, even in our difficult moments, that fidelity does its greatest work. Here, in the depths of our inner life, we learn to consummate Jesus' invitation to come, "drink."

"*And Drink*"

I had sought, Beloved,
my whole life to possess You,
in writings, in holy performing
and in endless wanting,
not grasping what it meant
to relent, to say yes—
then, finally, I exhaled into
being in one-anotherness;
this knowing that has become
our home of quenching love.

Chapter 8

Say Yes

*"Search me and know me
that all of me may know all of You,
even that which is within me,
that I don't yet know myself."*

Prayer Vol. 04

And so we now find ourselves entering the more unlanguageable and unseen movements of our intermingling with God. The work of Love in the deep self.

It's here, in our communion with God in our Dark Ocean, that we begin to truly drink, but it's also here where we face the darkness that is our own self. The deeper one goes into the ocean, the greater the pressure. There's no getting around the fact that it's the same in the soul. As we dive into God's presence and seek to draw water from the deeper places of His heart, we confront our need for control, for suffering avoidance, and for sense making within ourselves as well.

But what's true of the ocean's floor is true also of the soul, pressure produces fine pearls. Because when we finally do go deep with God, we discover some of the rarest gifts of intermingling life.

When we're reading Scripture, living Jesus' teaching, and learning to bring our mind into an experience of Truth, it feels like we have autonomy. But when it comes to the work of union in our Dark Ocean, we give that all up. We discover that we're at the mercy of Mercy. We are a kind of willfully blind, offering ourselves to the unexplainable yet trustworthy work of the Spirit.

As we do, we discover a new way of being, a way of affectionate consent. In this experience of communion we are more like a pregnant mother, carrying an unseen life that lives, breathes, imagines, and grows within her, and less like the captain of our own ship. We can only *let* the Spirit here, allowing His work and slowly learning what it means to lean in.

Our role in this deeper place is to say yes, to open up, to give ourselves to the project of being loved into who we're made to be in God's timing, and at His pace. That's not so intangible that we can't practise it, as we'll see, but our practices become about availability, not control. Willpower has no effect here, only a willingness to hold an unknowing trust will bear any fruit. Quietness and stillness become hallmarks of our prayer lives, our nature marked more now by godly acceptance rather than ambition.

As we turn our attention toward the mystery of our inner life, we hear the quiet yet persistent voice of Christ saying, "Here I am! I stand at the door and knock. If anyone hears my voice and opens the door, I will come in and eat with that person, and they with me."[64] And we dare begin opening up.

Here we discover that when it comes to the deepest parts of our being, it's not we who are knocking on the door of God's heart, but Christ who waits continually at the door of ours, longing to live in us in ever greater depths.

This sort of powerlessness, and opening up to God, isn't easy. Certainly not at first. It was over a decade into my communion with God before I was aware this kind of work was happening within me. I didn't come from a tradition that loved or valued the Spirit's soul-work like this, I had no vocabulary for it.

I used to think the idea of entering our Dark Ocean with the Spirit was overly sensitive nonsense. Ironic for an artist who had spent most of his life articulating his emotions and deeper senses through poetry and song. It had made sense to me in art, but in prayer I wasn't always able to see the connection between my Dark Ocean and my experience of God's presence. The denial didn't serve me well.

For years my prayer life consisted of a desperate loneliness. I wanted badly to live from the place of God's resident love, but I didn't know how. I could feel something was keeping me from depth, but I couldn't put my finger on what it was. Then, sitting in the window of a retreat centre on an autumn morning, warming in the sun, something profound happened.

I was reading a leadership book as part of my role on a church staff that explored some of the internal work that's become so common to me now but was so obscure back then. In one chapter, the author spoke about internal blind spots that hinder our experience of God's love. It encouraged the reader to take a moment and invite the Spirit to reveal to them anything from their past that was keeping them from an experience of God's love. I was cynical, cautious at the time of an overly therapeutic approach to Christian Spirituality. But out of respect for the author and the leadership team I was a part of, I decided to give it a quick go. I had nothing in my past I wasn't already aware of, the prayer would be brief and reassuring.

So, I opened my palms on my knees, took a deep breath, and prayed, "Lord, I want to know You more. Show me anything within me that keeps me from You." Instantly, and uncomfortably, the word *abandonment* gently impressed itself on my awareness. I was startled by it, I grew up in a loving middle-class suburban family. Abandonment? Not me.

But in the interest of staying faithful to the moment, I prayed again, "Holy Spirit, show me what this means." What followed was a short reel of my life experiences from childhood to present revealing a side of myself I'd never seen before.

When I was an eight-year-old child, my parents separated for a few short months. I remember very little about it—Mum's strength and kindness, Dad living somewhere else suddenly, their both affirming their unchanging love for us. I don't remember any painful feelings, but at the time of this prayer, my eldest was the same age I was then and it dawned on me that as amicable and loving as my parents were, this would have had a profound impact on me.

A few years later Mum became incredibly sick with a kind of chemical poisoning. Now, I do remember *that* being traumatic. She was strong, but her tears were unmissable and the diagnosis terrified me. We began learning sign language under the doctor's assumption she would go deaf. We children were afraid of losing her, if not to death then to the very real disconnection of illness.

Miraculously, and with a determined, hopeful resilience on Mum's part, she didn't get as bad as the doctors had promised. She even got better. But the fear of losing her was strong enough to have left its mark. These two events exposed my vulnerabilities.

Later, there was more. A terrible break-up with a teenage flame truly wrecked me, only serving to reinforce my fear that those we love may not stick around. Then, in my early twenties my first paid job at a church didn't go well either. I began working for a gifted pastor who I really looked up to but who, in their brokenness, pushed me away and slowly cut me out of ministry opportunities. It was an unjust situation, for sure, but a story was also developing deep down within me that only made it worse.

One of those events would have left its mark, but the Spirit was showing me that I'd interpreted all these experiences in one way— when I let people in, they hurt me. Throw in my sensitive, artistic nature and it's not difficult to see how I began to project onto God the sense that those I love could disappear at any time.

I didn't even have a difficult life. To me, these are very human and common experiences. They're nowhere near as bad as the tragic instances of abuse, trauma, and loss so many I've come to know and love have suffered. But to me, in my life with my temperament, they were enough to create a small deviation in my journey home to Love. A deviation the Spirit longed to heal.

That day as I sat with God seeing all this for the first time, I saw how all these little experiences led to my believing that *God* would abandon me at any time. I'd made Him in the image of my hurt. Without knowing it I treated Him as someone who could leave at a whim. Someone to whom if I gave away my deepest longings had the power to wield them against me.

When I was doing well, God was with me. When I wasn't performing, He was poised to leave or disown me. I'd built a doorway within myself between God and me. I'd put up a sign reading "keep out," and buried the memory.

And now, Christ was knocking.

That day, as I invited Him to heal my soul, I sensed Him moving there, doing something. I wasn't instantly healed of my sense of abandonment, but knowing it existed empowered me to draw nearer to God when I felt it. The Spirit has been setting me free to receive His love without fear ever since.

THE ROOMS OF US

We could imagine our souls as a living mansion with many rooms. Before we awaken to Divine Love, we have lived without power our whole lives. There's been no lights to navigate, no heat to warm it. We've been walking around blind, considering it normal, doing our best to decorate and live in the place we've been put. We develop coping mechanisms and ways of operating that have made our lives livable, and over time we've come to call it flourishing, because we haven't known any different.

But it's clunky and out of whack. In reality, our mansion is more of a prison.

Then one day, Christ appears to us, standing outside. He is pure, beautiful light, and suddenly all the rooms, hallways, and spaces facing outside are lit up with Him. For the first time we begin to see ourselves as we really are, we experience God meeting our thirst, our need for awakening and healing.

In this first experience of Him our lives start their transformation. We wrestle with the changes needed to follow Him, often addressing the surface behaviours that are most obvious to us. We clean the windows, sweep the floors of our outer rooms, and are able to begin getting our house in order.

But there's still work to be done, we need to let Christ *into* the house. Light must penetrate deeper if it's to get rid of the mildew that has grown in the dark and cold. Because there are many more inner rooms that not even we've entered in a long time, and years of lightless care have rendered them rotten and unlivable.

But Jesus is considerate, and He knows that this will be very hard for us. He doesn't barge in, He stands at the door knocking. This kind of work requires consent because Love never forces itself upon anyone. He is kind, gentle, and protecting of our dignity, He never intrudes. And so He stands there knocking at our front door, asking that He may bring His renewing light further inward to us.

Here Christ comes to satisfy our thirst for the continued healing work of the salvation of our being. He wants in so He can renovate, liberate, and clean what's been left without light for so long.

But something's happened to us, we've realised that in the darkness our house has become a mess. To confront it now is an overwhelming, even painful prospect. The moment we awaken to grace we have a simultaneous revelation of our living conditions. The walls of our inner room are smeared with grease we didn't know was there, dust has collected on the furniture, bathrooms are messy and half-cleaned. Letting Christ in means facing it all, including the shame we've tried so hard to ignore.

We didn't realise when Christ first showed up that we'd someday have to deal with all this. We'd hoped salvation was more sanitary, easy, miraculous, and external. More like buying a new home than the hard work of renovating. Now we're confronted with the harsh reality of the long-term work and the risky vulnerability of letting God in. What if He's put off? What if He's offended or can't love the rottenness of the rest of the mansion of my soul? How will I survive the pain of facing that which I've sought to forget?

I have found time and time again that for many of us the response to Christ's longing to come, if we're honest with ourselves, is a resounding "No!" We're happy with our moralism, with the sense that we're saved *from* whatever it is we were afraid of. We're happy too with our intellectualism and the sense of goodness that comes from Christian community and our newfound access to truth. But when it comes to the deeper works, we recoil.

God longs to drink of our deep places, but we deny Him. As much as we long for communion, this work is just too hard, too confronting.

And so our addictions, our wounds, abandonments, fears, and anxieties remain untouched. We shuffle around in the garden outside, maybe even throw a new lick of paint on the odd wall, but the real stuff of who we are, the stuff deep down, remains full of mould and dampness. The pores of which still fill the house. Yes we feel some light, but we keep getting ill inwardly. We keep feeling as though Love is at arm's-length.

But there is a way out, or *in*. We can move toward vulnerability. We can open up the doorways of our anxiety, fear, shame, and guilt, our anger, lust, jealousy, and doubt, and allow Him in.

We can say yes.

The image of Christ knocking on the doors of us in Revelation reminds us that God is the initiator. It is He who persists, wants, and acts continually in the direction of soul-intimacy with us, regardless of the condition of our hearts.

Here our usual assumptions about God are flipped on their head. Because we so often believe that it's He who is distant from us, receding or withdrawing, when in fact it's *He* who "has come to seek ... that which was lost,"[65] who chases us to the ends of the earth, even into death,[66] and *we* who are perpetually running.

As it turns out, the barriers to satiating our *dis*-ease, our thirst in God, aren't on His end but ours. We are the ones holed up within ourselves, unsure how to allow all this ache to pour into the God we desperately want.

This is understandable, we live in a world naturally threatening to vulnerability. As we grow and live, we collect experiences of hurt, of being told we're not lovable or worthy. There are both those who harm out of anger and willfulness and those who hurt us out of their own woundedness. Either way, it doesn't take long before we've experienced enough to tell us that the world and many of the people in it aren't always safe.

These experiences cause us to build doors in front of our deepest places, but so does bad theology. Many of us really struggle to see this pursuing and thirsting God in the biblical story. For too many years we've heard about the judgemental God, the one who divides, supports wars, is continually poised to tell us how wrong we are. We've heard preaching that speaks of God's holiness without His compassion, His judgement without His patience, His truth without His love.

It's right to revere God, but much of this makes us afraid of Him instead. Letting Him in, then, is more terrifying than liberating. I've met many, many Christians in my life who feel this way, but if the God we worship is too scary to let in to our shames, guilts, fears, and vulnerabilities, then He's not the knocking Christ of Revelation 3:20. He's not the God I see decimating our need for inner doorways, wanting to simply eat together.

Finally, there's ignorance too. Maybe we haven't even considered this image of Jesus knocking on the doorways of our souls. We're not aware that we all build walls based on our upbringing, our family of origin, our theology culture or experience. A painful majority of Christians aren't aware of their Dark Ocean or how to access it. For those of us who live that way, we simply don't let Christ in because we're not self-aware. We don't know there are doors, let alone how to open them. I suspect this is the majority of us. I know it was true for me for the first half of my Christian life.

For many of us we, too, need to ask God to reveal our historical blind spots.

We're not told in Revelation that Jesus wants in so He can clean us up, judge us, pour contempt on our inabilities, or tell us that our disordered thirsts offend Him. We're told He wants in so He can satisfy His own thirst for communion with us. Or as Christ Himself puts it, so that we can eat together. Not with physical food, but with the food of love, goodness, beauty, and truth. The spiritual food of communion.

This is the sharing of desires, the offering of a being-level nakedness with one another. Christ knocks at the doorway of our hearts so He can come and live within us, warming us from inside, being one with us, marrying our souls forever.

This promise is the living invitation beneath all our individual realities. No matter what you're doing or who you are, Christ is knocking at the door of your soul. Have you done unthinkable things? Right there, Christ is knocking. Are you numb, burnt out, cynical? Christ is knocking there too. Are you anxious, depressed, and afraid? There in the very essence of your pain Jesus is thirsting for you. Whatever the door, He is there, unphased and undaunted, just asking you to open up to His love.

Close your eyes.

Breathe deeply.

Open up your deep self.

With all your being, say *yes*.

CURIOUS LIVING

Discovering that I had been projecting a deep-seated fear of abandonment onto God in our communion that day, I began a journey of prayerful curiosity. I decided that every time I felt disconnected from God, or as if He was unhappy or withdrawing from me, I would interrogate my feelings to see which story they lined up with, "Is this really God, or am *I* closing this door?"

As I did, reactions to God and others in my life slowly demystified and I was able to open up more and more to the idea that God never leaves. I saw how, actually, I was often the one withdrawing from God as a preventative measure, to beat Him to it so I wouldn't be disappointed. Instead of turning toward Him in my failure and pain (a practice we'll explore in the next chapter), I turned away to self-isolation.

Becoming curious of my reactions and responses to God and to the deeper feelings within me, I began to experience Him more and more where I'd felt empty and alone before. That's the power of consent, we can learn to quench our thirst in the very places we've been self-dehydrating.

By learning to listen to the movements of our souls, and becoming curious about them, we can slowly diagnose and open the doors we build within ourselves. Do we arrive home from a social event feeling desperately lonely? Do we reach for a drink after each workday as a way of unwinding and finding peace? Do we get angry at other people who don't live up to our moral standards? Each of these is an opportunity to stop and ask the Holy Spirit, "Why do I feel this ache?" and "How do I turn to You and let You meet it?"

The purpose isn't to see and solve an issue immediately, but to learn to, as we live through our responses to the world, experience them *with* God. Communion, and the transformation that it brings, slowly takes hold there and God's presence becomes more constant to us.

There are thousands of these little cues every day if we're listening. They are the knocks of Love in the doorways we've built. They can be more subtle too, of course, like jealous thoughts, voices within that tell us we're not enough, a perpetual numbness of heart or a disguised but persistent anxiety. At each door Christ knocks, asking, "Will you let Me in here so we can talk it through? Will you let Me sit with you in this moment?"

We can discern whether the voice is God's or someone else's by whether it convicts or condemns. The Spirit is in the convicting business[67] and is commissioned by God to guide us into truth.[68] But the voice of the enemy only wants to destroy and condemn.[69] The voice of conviction brings an awareness of something that needs to be healed, transformed, or abandoned. Condemnation tells us we're the problem and that we're a hopeless failure.

Conviction says, "You're doing wrong here," condemnation says, "You as a person are wrong." The voice of the Spirit will bring with it the grace and courage to go the journey with God and will feel like an invitation into love. The voice of condemnation will drive us into the shadows and tempt us to give up and keep on with the disorder we know.

The experience of saying yes should feel more like spiritual unclenching than willful straining. When we notice ourselves pent up and struggling to receive the reality of God's love, we simply need to take a few deep breaths, become aware of God's presence, and consent again to Love.

You may even like to visualise Jesus knocking on the doorway of your heart, longing to sit at the table of your soul, speaking healing words of love, naming for you the door that prevents His arrival. You might imagine opening up and seeing what conversation takes place there.

The gospel isn't a story so much of our pursuit of God, but of God's pursuit of us. Of His *thirst* for us. Time after time, when we've turned away to far lesser things, God hasn't contented Himself with detachment and disappointment, but has pursued us. All through the story He goes to incredible lengths to love us, the culmination of which is the gift and ultimate offering of His Son.

In reality, we don't yet fully know ourselves. In our many-roomedness, we can't always see the doorways of self-protection we've built in response to our wrong beliefs or negative experiences of the world. We can't see what we can't see. So God takes us by the hand, leading us into our deep self, liberating us from our fears.

We can't do it alone, we need His light. We need to invite Him to speak to us gently, to show us what we can't see, and to eat with us there until we're more full of His presence than our fears and brokenness. To do so is to enter a life of rest, of being led to the waters, of learning to be open so that God can do the transforming work.

A life of holy-allowing.

But to drink deeply of Love we have to go further still, not only into past experiences that build barriers within us, but into our very real and *present* suffering. We're invited to pray our pain.

Chapter 9

Praying the Pain

> *"The deepest road*
> *is the road toward,*
> *not away, from the*
> *aches of my existence."*
>
> Prayer Vol. 04

Thirst itself is a longing for what we *don't* have, what's incomplete. So, to touch our thirst is to face the pain of our unfulfilled longings, and the suffering inherent with a broken world.

This world dehydrates us, it's what sin and disorder do. Be it lost dreams, sickness, death and grief, busyness, financial stress, a broken heart, a broken family, political divisiveness, or mental health, the wear on our souls mounts up. We thirst because we live in a world where these things aren't the exception, but the rule. If we can't turn to God for water in their midst, if we can't allow Him to love us in these experiences, we'll shrivel up spiritually.

But often, that's not what we do. When we feel the acute pain of our longing and disappointments, we're more likely to turn toward things that promise immediate relief, like scrolling, streaming, or eating, rather than self-reflection. Or to the emotional extremes of jealousy, anxiety, lust, or rage rather than honest, vulnerable prayer.

Anything to avoid pain rather than feel it.

These responses are often so natural to us that they hardly register. Sometimes we may not even consciously feel the pain so much as the relief or high we get from online shopping, staying up late streaming a series, watching pornography, or drinking. Our inability to feel our pain gives our addictions more power than they deserve.

At other times, our pain can be so conscious and severe it feels like we'll explode, or melt, like our very soul is dying within our bodies. In those heated moments we convince ourselves that all we can do is numb, medicate, or distract ourselves to survive. Deep down we know it won't. We can't stop the sunrise. Tomorrow morning we'll only wake to find our unaddressed pain still with us like an existential hangover.

If we continue on like this, eventually hopelessness begins to creep in.

On the other end of the spectrum to active numbing, is shutting down where, instead of distracting ourselves or medicating on the things of the world, we slam the lid shut completely in the hope of killing desire altogether. Maybe then, if we can turn down the volume on thirsting at all, it won't hurt so much when it's unfulfilled.

Heartbreak does that. Losing someone we love can tempt us to shut ourselves away from future love altogether in the hope of protecting what we've discovered is so profoundly vulnerable. We withdraw, create safe barriers, maybe even develop a prickly exterior so that no one is tempted to get close enough to harm us. All the while not realising we're doing the same to God in the process. Because who is more threatening to our deepest longing than the one who is most posed to fulfil it?

When we shut down, life becomes tasteless. In choosing to not feel pain, we find ourselves not feeling anything. We feel no joy, excitement, hope, or energy too. We become grey, so does the world, and our prayer life dies with it. Eventually, enough time passes that we forget why and how we became this way. Like living with the symptoms of a long-lost diagnosis.

The world is a painful place, and you and I are going to experience it whether we like it or not. Undoubtedly, you know exactly what I'm talking about. You may even find yourself in the words you've just read. I have, which is why it's so easy to describe. I know what it's like to experience the weight of unbearable pain and to do anything but face it.

I also know what it's like to bring it all Home.

By the time I'd reached my mid-twenties I found myself locking up. I'd started the decade with a rare zeal for a life of ministry and a romanticism for how it would look. I was beaming with a passion to do the work of the kingdom and to give my life away. But I got a job a few years in for a church that took the wind out of my sails.

My boss was a gifted man, but a flawed one too. I was only on staff with him for a year, but by the end of it I was having panic attacks on the way to work every day.

In that short time I experienced the full weight of a difficult leader. I was yelled at, condescended, accused of planning a church schism, and, after serving as a volunteer at both services every Sunday for three years and doing the church network's years-long ministry training course, among all the extras, was still told I wasn't doing enough to be a leader.

In the end, after gaining the courage to honestly confront them about their regular angst toward me, I was told that not only was I making it all up, I was also clearly not cut out for, or called to, ministry. It hurt, and it felt like the end of my calling.

I think the reason it was so disorienting was because he was also a loving and kind person both toward me and others too. No one is the sum only of their shadows, and he certainly wasn't. But there was no denying the impact he had on me as a young, impression-able man. Someone I looked up to, someone with seeming spiritual authority, making out I was no good for that which I deeply longed for, had a huge effect on me.

The whole experience emptied me. I bowed out as best I could, blaming myself for not making it work, and lived with the devastation that my hope of doing ministry was crushed. It mat-tered to me so much precisely because it was my deepest desire to work with God in full-time vocational ministry. It was the ultimate rejection, in the most painful way, in my most vulnerable longing.

That wasn't the first crisis I'd faced, but as a young man it was the one that collected much of my other feelings of failure and rejection. It was what brought my other unacknowledged inner work to the surface for the first time. I wouldn't have told you I was depressed, but looking back, it was probably true. I was struggling to feel things, to have zeal and energy. I would tell Katie it felt as if someone had thrown a concrete blanket over me.

I loved God deeply, but I didn't know how to reckon with my pain and it was killing me spiritually.

I can't for the life of me remember why I began this particular practice, but around that time I started prayer journaling. I do remember that it arose from my recognition that I was waking up in pain every day. Both from these experiences and my early journey with chronic illness.

Mornings were the hardest for me, they felt repetitive and hopeless. If I wasn't careful, my mind, racing by breakfast time, would lead to anxiety that would be almost impossible to get rid of the rest of the day. As a way of facing it, and because I was often too fatigued to pray in my mind, I would take myself to a café as soon as I woke up and write my prayers.

By write my prayers, I mean something more like aching through words. Line by line I would allow the pain of my soul to pour out in ink toward God. I would articulate the heaviness, the sadness, the grief, and the fear, often surprised at what I was reading as I wrote.

I would write about my anxiety, my numbness, my need for love. I would ask God where He was and what He had to say about me. In short, I began to explore and enter my pain, with God.

Looking back, it sounds so obvious, but as a young man who was still discovering his own Dark Ocean, it was revolutionising. I'd never considered sharing my pain with God so honestly. I had been brought up thinking it was irreverent to be as honest, and brutal, as I was. But here I was just opening right up, and finding God's compassionate understanding there.

I'd been reading the Psalms too, appreciating their own brutal honesty. And I noticed something, they never held any punches toward God, they were shameless in their transparency about their emotions and condition, but they almost always ended with a declaration of refusal to lose hope, "Put your hope in God," they would tell their souls, "for I will yet praise him, my Saviour and my God."[70] I could spend an hour pouring out the sorrow of my soul, but I made sure I always ended in trust, in hope, in anticipation that God is good, true, and that He cares.

The word *compassion* literally means "to suffer together." That's what I experienced those mornings. I shared, He listened, we sat there together. I didn't get answers, I got God's quiet, subtle but noticeable presence and a slow liberation from my numbness. I learned that God cares about my pain, that He wants to hear it, that He prefers honesty over performance. I found that after spending an hour or so writing out what was in my soul, I felt lighter, freer, loved.

What I stumbled into was my first taste of experiencing pain *in* God. Later I would learn to find this place without pen and paper, but for now, it was profound for me to discover that when it comes to knowing my Beloved, my pain isn't a barrier, but a gift.

Slowly, my shutting down turned into a new opening up. Life and joy began to return, my spirit was renewed, and God became more close than I'd ever known Him. I couldn't see it then, but my desperately writing prayers every morning was soon to become my vocation. What felt like the graveyard of ministry would become the garden bed of new life. Writing would become my offering to the world.

I hold no grudge or hurt today, and I've had beautiful moments of reconciliation with some of the elders of that church since. In fact, in the years following I would have a redemptive experience of church community and church leadership working on staff at a local Vineyard church. I experienced humility and vitality there, compassion, and care as we all sought the face of God together. I believe in God's presence and the importance of local church community more than I ever have, even in the face of the public figure let-downs of these past years. For me, this part of my story isn't about the church, it's about learning the gift of pain.

PAIN, A GIFT

In a famous prediction about the life of Jesus, the prophet Isaiah said, "He was despised and rejected by mankind, a man of suffering, and familiar with pain."[71] It's no small comfort to hear that

Jesus Himself knows pain, knows the ache of an unmet thirst in the place it matters most. Like many of us, He's experienced what it's like to live not just a moment, but a whole life of grief.

But there has also never been a more joyful, peaceful, loving, and vital human being in all of history, which tells me that pain and the presence of God are not opposing forces. If Jesus can be a man of sorrow and be simultaneously the embodiment of peace and joy, then hidden in our life in Him is the same invitation.

I've heard it said that the crucifixion isn't only something God *did*, but who He *is*. Meaning, God loves like the cross—self-sacrificially, with humility, amidst grief and pain, and with compassionate love. That really spoke to me, because on the cross I see God willingly entering our suffering and turning it into love. There, experiencing the ultimate pain, Jesus invites us to see what it's like to sit with, rather than avoid, it. Not only that, but to experience pain as anticipating resurrection. To sit with it in hope.

In the cross we're shown that the way to healing is *through* the crucifixions we experience in this life—the loss of a loved one, the persistent depression and anxiety, our sexual struggles, abandonment, boredom, or fear. Right there in our pain, we suffer with God on the cross. We experience what He experienced, and He grieves with us.

In the Man of Sorrows we're invited not to avoid or shut down in our pain, but to experience it, together.

The New Testament authors seemed to know this well, because we find them making bizarre statements about suffering being *good* for us like, "Consider it pure joy, my brothers and sisters, whenever you face trials of many kinds," "We rejoice in our sufferings," "If you should suffer for what is right, you are blessed,"[72] and of course Jesus Himself in the Sermon on the Mount considers the mourner, the hungry, the persecuted, to be best positioned for His kingdom.

The apostles frequently see suffering and trials not as an aberration but the very vehicle through which we discover perseverance, character, and love. What James called "maturity."

If we were meant to assume Jesus' crucifixion would relieve us of our own, no one told the early church. They saw it as baked into our journey as Christians, as something to be embraced. That's not very popular today. If in your intense pain I wrote you an email saying, "Be stoked! This one's going to bear great fruit," you'd likely cancel me. But if I'm honest, few things have helped me experience the true *in*ness of God like my pain. It truly is a gift.

My intention here isn't to offer a theology of pain, or to speak generally about how to get through it, but to explore what it means for communing with Divine Love. With satisfying our thirst for living *in* Him amidst it. We are going to experience the pain of our thirst persistently in this life. We can't avoid it, but we can pray it.

If we'll allow it, pain can actually drive us directly into a divine experience of God in our deep self. Because the deeper and more powerful the ache, the greater and more profound the possibility of experiencing God there is.

THE ADDICT, THE STOIC, AND THE MYSTIC

In his book *Fill These Hearts*, theologian Christopher West explores three ways we try to satisfy or relieve the ache of our thirst in this world. I found it really helpful language for naming the responses we have when pain visits us and a hopeful paradigm for learning to turn toward God amidst it. West personalises these responses as the *Addict*, the *Stoic*, and the *Mystic*. The first, and in our times most common, way we often deal with our deep thirst is by becoming what West calls "the *Addict*." The Addict is the person who simply tries to feed their desires on the world, forever giving in to them, perpetually unsatisfied. The Addict either consciously or unconsciously believes that just another drink, relationship, party, promotion, or success will bring them the internal rest they pine for.

Underneath the ideology of the Addict is the "follow our hearts" and "live my truth" rhetorics. Both would say that true happiness is found in pursuing what we want and obtaining it at any cost, rather than through any kind of denial or transformation.

Ultimately, the Addict way of living seeks satisfaction here, in this world. It taunts and tempts us that just around the corner of the next overseas trip, raise, house purchase, or sexual expedition is happiness and contentment. It's this lie that marketing agencies, self-help gurus, and the global economy itself rely on to keep us buying.

The name says it all, feeding our thirsts in the hope of satisfying them only forms an addiction to them. This dependence gives whatever we use power over us and we lose ourselves in the pursuit.

Then, there's the *Stoic*. The Stoic instead pushes their thirst down, denying themselves it's vitality, and ultimately ending up sleepwalking through life. The Stoic convinces themselves it's better not to feel at all, that this particular human power is untrustworthy and needs to be subdued so it's never felt again. The Stoic doesn't have a vision for a redeemed longing. They've given up on the idea that spirituality, or even life itself, can be vital, romantic, and energising. Because if it is, the temporal shortfall is too much to bear.

Instead, their flame is starved of oxygen until it eventually snuffs. Numbness creeps in and prayer becomes onerous, unimaginative, and dutiful. The Stoic eventually looks at life with a kind of hopeless resignation. They lose the ability to believe in change. Religion is a framework. Right and wrong are paramount. They eventually give up on the hope of ever feeling fully alive again.

If the Addict is our eros gone rogue, abusing beauty, goodness, and truth for self gain, the Stoic is all truth, no beauty, and a narrow moralised vision for goodness.

The Stoic plays down personal experience of God, of change, of genuine transformation. They shut themselves off from pleasure because they're afraid of it, afraid of losing control of themselves. They feel that there's no life in their communion with God, faith becomes a chore, an exercise in obedience and theology. There's no longer any adventure to God's love.

Really, there's a Stoic and an Addict in all of us, and we can be both at different times of our lives in different ways. Because human beings tend to be creatures of extremes, and we despise discomfort. Addict and Stoic are just two names we give to the disorder inherent with our fallen nature. Thank God those aren't the only responses to our deep thirst. There's a third way.

A way that can become our home.

The way, West tells us, of the *Mystic*.

"The *Mystic*," we discover, "is the one who allows himself to feel the deepest depths of human desire and chooses to 'stay with the pain' of wanting more than this life has to offer."[73] The word *mystic* often gets a bad rap in our times, but a Christian mystic is simply someone who believes in the centrality of the experience of God's love, through prayer, for every Christian who seeks it. Christian mysticism isn't an Eastern-borrowed faux Christianity but the very living *in*ness Jesus promised us. At the heart of it, the Mystic is someone who brings their thirst to God. Who believes only He can satisfy it.

It's incredibly tempting to either turn away or give in to the deep aches dwelling within us—I know, like you, from experience. It's one thing when we're talking about eating too much sugar or getting stuck on social media. But what about our longing for a lover or our substance addictions? What about our perpetual self-hatred, depression, or chronic anxiety? What about these forms of pain that are overwhelming and consuming and don't go away in weeks, months, or years, if they ever even do?

Turning toward God in these moments, in these continued aches, is what West tells us the Mystic gives their lives to. I wholeheartedly believe this is what the psalmist means when he says, "My whole being longs for you in a dry and parched land."[74] Yes, he's thirsting physically and that's crucial. But that's not ultimately humanity's greatest pain. The deepest cut is existential.

The psalmist feels our painful longing for a child, a soulmate, a different body, or our physical healing. Maybe his thirsting isn't just a romantic, prayerful thirsting, but a bone-deep desperation for God to be big enough and satisfying enough to fill those great gaping holes he has in his life. What the psalmist's cry teaches us is that it's in the midst of our struggle, not either side of it, that our longing for God is most articulate.

The Mystic, like the psalmist, has woken up to the limitations of the world and ceases to look to it as the source of its potential satisfaction. They give themselves instead to prayer, to abiding in their vows to God, to anticipating the coming consummation of all things.

For us as Mystics, God Himself becomes our "beauty for ashes, joy for the mourner, oil of gladness, and garment of praise."[75] He can and even may take away the pain altogether, but that's not ultimately our hope. Our hope is that God will transform us through it, that we will have a cruciform experience, that we'll learn to live simultaneously on the cross of vulnerable love and in the empty tomb of joy and healing until our Lord destroys death and pain altogether and resurrection is our permanent reality.

Some years ago, in the depth of winter here in our home beside the beach, while a storm rolled in from the Pacific East, pummeling our home, I had an encounter like this that eventually became the seed for this book.

I was unwell again, and three months in, when I was deeply fatigued by the experience I found myself oscillating between the Stoic and the Addict. I spent day and night, near comatose in my living-room reading chair, bored, frustrated, and reckoning with the disappointment I felt over years of lost life and the disconnection it brought to my family and community.

Some days, I dealt with it by gorging on Netflix series to avoid the boredom and disappointment I was feeling. On others I would try to shut down desire altogether in a kind of fatalistic acceptance of my lot. I reasoned that my pain was coming from the fact that I *expected* life to be something different, something better. Maybe if I gave up on the hope of vitality I would find inner peace.

Neither approach fruited anything good. The former was just junk food for the soul, the latter only numbed. They both made it worse.

Then, one night, as I picked up my laptop to watch a show, I felt the Spirit gently speaking, "Son, stop. Let's sit together. Let Me feel your pain with you." I was exhausted and empty, the last thing I felt like doing was praying, but I also knew that what I was doing wasn't working either. I was finally ready to open up.

So, I put aside my laptop, closed my eyes, took a few deep breaths, and opened myself toward God. Then I did something I'd been avoiding: I faced my pain. But this time, I did it *with* God, in my deep self.

It was brutal. It hurt. I wept. I let it all hang out and just imagined God seeing it and beholding me there. I grieved over my lost dreams, over my deadness of heart, my isolation and sickness.

I didn't say words, I just held it there, *in* God.

I let Him have it, and I asked Him to stay with me.

What followed was a rollercoaster experience. Over the course of the prayer I oscillated between grief and peace, anger and calm and a sense of God's loving presence. It wasn't easy, but I stuck with *feeling* the pain of it and directed it toward Love. I simply prayed, "God, deep down it's You I want. All this thirsting is for You. You are my desire, You are the centre of it all, and I know You care for me." I was directing my thirst toward God, giving Him a chance to quench my deep self.

We stayed there together, God and I, beholding each other in the wrestle.

By the end, we were closer.

And my soul was still.

I had liberated my thirst, in Love.

FOLLOWING THE PAIN

This is the invitation we have in the Spirit, the inner experience of pain not only *with,* but *in* God. It's not easy to articulate, but it begins with us feeling our pain right in our depths and experiencing it there with Him. That requires a willingness to feel our pain when it comes. It means making room in our lives instead of giving in to the reflex to numb ourselves on the world around us.

That doesn't mean we have to run headlong into overwhelm, only that we need to grow a gentle consciousness of what underneath us is motivating our disorder. Because not all pain is obvious, some is subtle, hiding its volume beneath the little reactions in our daily lives.

One of the ways we can foster this awareness is by being curious about our reactions to others or God in those little moments. In my own life I call this "following the pain." The way I do this is by reflecting on moments where I overreact with others, feel irrationally anxious, or am offended by someone or something easily. Paying attention, I open a note on my phone and go through the following stages.

I begin by noting the experience, describing in detail what happened. I overreacted about a small comment someone made, I got angry quickly at the kids over something trivial, I was anxious all day after receiving a text or email. I don't hold back, but honestly describe my response and disorder in that moment.

Then, I ask myself why. I start by jotting down what I can make sense of myself and then turn to the Spirit for help, asking Him to show me what deeper pain lies beneath this seemingly trivial detail. I sit there, listening and being aware of any words, images, or memories that arise as I pray. I'm amazed at how often I'll see something I'd never recognized before, a connection with something residing deeper down.

Was my reaction to the kids based out of a feeling of shame I have about my shortfalls as a father? Am I anxious about that text because I don't like conflict? Did I make that comment about how good my friend's life is because I'm secretly living in disappointment about an element of my own? All these are the thirsts that dwell within me, waiting to be brought to light in the love of God.

Finally, I finish by considering my response, and the ways I can move toward healing. All this I do not in a spirit of criticism and insecurity, but in the presence of God and in prayer. I try to do it in God, experiencing His compassion. The more I do it, the more I'm able to keep watching over my surface behaviours and live in the healing of the Spirit in the deeper ones.

Then, in the moments when the pain I feel is peaking and I'm overwhelmed, I take a few deep breaths and open my deep self again to God. I meditate on our intermingling, on His co-suffering love, and I invite Him in to sit with me. There, in communion, I remember His promise to intercede within me in unlanguaged groans beyond comprehension, and I rest in those.

I let God pray for me, within me. I say *yes*.

It's my returning continually to this experience that has built my pain into a place of communion with God. It's where I quench my thirst for healing, for relief from the persistent reality of living in a broken world. There, in the darkness of me, I've discovered powerful joy, rich love, and the unceasing gaze of the Yearning.

This practice of turning toward God in our pain is simple, but that doesn't mean it's easy. It's a commitment to—instead of picking up our phone, lashing out in anger, pouring another drink, or entering that URL—choose to sit with God in our discomfort and pain.

It could be over something as benign as boredom, or as intense as habitual lust. It could be amidst the constant ache of the loss of a loved one, or the grief over not having one at all. It's simply our, as often as we can remember, turning the attention of our heart toward God and affording Him the opportunity to suffer it *with* us.

As an intentional practice, it may mean taking a few minutes aside when the feelings are most intense to posture ourselves in prayer or, like me, following the hints of our surface living toward the deeper currents of our embedded hurts. Above all, though, it's the decision to see pain as an opportunity to move toward liberation rather than an obstacle to prayer.

It's to, with a cruciform heart, bring it into Love.

Over time, as we continue to return to God in our moments of pain, we will, like a wilting plant regularly watered again, begin to flourish. New shoots of hope and animation will enter where only dead leaves had lined the branches, and we will begin to experience the transformation of God's eternal, present love.

Our pain becoming the very place of our greatest transformation.

Sometimes, to thirst is to suffer. Because thirst is predicated in our need, our lack. In this world where spiritual water is rare, it's only in opening up our pain to a Love who promises healing that we can experience true freedom.

Chapter 10

Naked Presence

"Fearless faith,
is allowing God's love
into our worst parts,
and running no longer."

Prayer Vol. 04

As we begin to open ourselves up to the work of the Spirit moving in us, we're invited into a whole new way of understanding our own living transparently before Him, our nakedness. Nakedness is our original state in the story of creation. Not only physically, but emotionally, mentally, and spiritually too. We could call it our *seen*ness.

When Genesis tells us that "Adam and his wife were both naked, and they felt no shame,"[76] it's speaking to both an external and internal reality. The very reason we could be naked was that we felt no shame. The reason we felt no shame was because we'd only ever experienced secure relationship. First with God, and then because of that primary experience, with each other.

We knew no other way. We lived fearlessly, but naively, in a positive sense. We had only experienced perfect security and because of it weren't eyes wide open to the true magnitude of our insufficiency. Like young children who feel bold and brave in the security of their parents, we were yet to awaken to just how needy we truly were. We felt shameless precisely because we didn't yet know what shame was.

But we would soon learn.

In the meantime we're told in Genesis 3:8 that Adam and Eve "heard the sound of the LORD God as he was walking in the garden in the cool of the day." Notice that our infant relationship with God, as pure as it was, was still an external one. We were yet to experience the inner intermingling, the fullness of the divine life we were made for.

How can we know? Because Paul tells us in Ephesians that our being *in* God (the gift of the Spirit in and through Christ) isn't plan B, but that "he [God] chose us in him [Christ] *before* the creation of the world ... predestined us for adoption to sonship through Jesus Christ."[77] He says it again in 2 Timothy 1:9, "This grace was given us in Christ Jesus *before* the beginning of time." Peter also teaches us this, saying, "He was chosen *before* the creation of the world, but was revealed in these last times for your sake."[78] Being filled internally and welcomed *into* God was always the plan.

So in the garden we were naked, but it wasn't a mature nakedness. The hope was that we would trust God and walk with Him, slowly maturing and choosing love, awaiting this gift of His Son and

His indwelling Spirit. That our awareness of our insufficiency would grow up beside our experience of security in trinitarian love.

But that's not what happened. A crisis occurred. We tried self-sufficiency instead. Disorder entered. We fell sick with sin.

Immediately after, the Bible tells, Adam's and Eve's "eyes were opened, and they suddenly felt shame at their nakedness."[79] Our nakedness which had been a sign and symbol of our emotional and spiritual liberty now became our very cause of shame and anxiety. Where being *seen* by God had once been what made us free, now it was our source of terror.

Now that we knew our insufficiency we no longer wanted to be seen. In sin, our *other*-security became *in*security. And when we encountered God next, what did we do? We "hid from [Him] among the trees of the garden."[80]

We've been hiding ever since.

HIDING HURTS

Hiding is what we do when we're guilty. Fugitives hide, so do children when they break their mother's favourite vase. But hiding doesn't solve anything. We're no less guilty of something by running from the consequences. In fact, running only makes it worse, delaying the inevitable facing-up that comes when we're found.

In my second year of high school whilst my parents were away on a weekend trip with my older brother, I convinced my cousins to skip school with me to drink the rum they'd pilfered from a party the weekend before. I drank half a bottle of rum, smoked an entire pack of cigarettes, and proceeded to vomit so regularly, for such a long period of time, that on arriving home from their trip, my parents threatened to take me to the hospital for a stomach pump. With no confidence I could pull one over the doctors if my parents followed through on the threat, I confessed everything. I was duly grounded, spent two days clawing my way out of the nausea and tried to move on with my life.

The problem was, I couldn't. To cover my tracks at school I had told my form teacher I'd taken the day off sick. That would have been enough for most teachers, but not Mr. Beckett. He was militant with his discipline and ran an unforgivingly strict classroom. He once sent my friend Mike home on a mufti day because his fluro yellow T-shirt was too bright. True story.

Day after day Mr. Beckett kept asking for a letter from my parents, but I didn't have one. I didn't have one because I knew they wouldn't cover for me. They hated lying and were big on integrity. They would force another confession. A confession that would only mean one thing, reprisals.

The guilt consumed me. It kept me up at night, and set me on edge all day at school. I dreaded seeing Mr. Beckett and dodged him like a shadow as best I could through every class hallway. But every morning began the same, "Strahan, where's that note?" Eventually I told my parents and, as expected, they sent me in the next day with a self-written letter of confession and apology.

Feeling assured of certain death, I walked into class the next day and handed it over without saying a word. There was silence. Then, with a deep sigh and a solemn face he looked up and said only one sentence, "I'm not angry, Strahan, I'm just disappointed that you lied to me." He was genuinely hurt that a thirteen-year-old boy had lied about wagging school. Mr. Beckett had a soft side, it seemed. He took it personally. I was duly rebuffed and sent off to the form dean. It was all over in a minute.

I'd spent a whole week feeling sick, hardly sleeping, living in anxiety and hiding, when only a brief moment of awkward honesty would have made it go away in an instant. That's the irrational power of hiding. It steals from us for no other reason than our delirious belief that we'll feel better if we're not fully seen. If we don't confront our shame.

Aren't we the same with God? We pretend as though we can hide what feels most ugly or unwanted within us by ignoring it or doing our best to run away, but He sees it anyway. We may confess with our mouths that God sees all and loves us anyway, but functionally, when we give in to anger, lust, to addiction or to something else, we act as though He's not there.

We may piously pray with the author of Psalm 139, "You know when I sit and when I rise; you perceive my thoughts from afar. You discern my going out and my lying down; you are familiar with all my ways. Before a word is on my tongue you, LORD, know it completely,"[81] but when it comes to being seen in our shame and guilt, we hide away, living like it's not true.

Pretending doesn't change how bad we feel, nor God's desire to love and know us, all it does is prolong the pain, and grieve God's pursuing heart. And so, He knocks.

This dawned on me early in my faith. I began to notice the way I would avoid anything spiritual when I felt as though I had, or was, failing in some area. Deep down I believed God saw and knew it all, that He saw my failure before it even happened, but I convinced myself that avoiding facing it with Him would make the feelings of guilt more palpable. Theologically I agreed with the psalmist, functionally, I didn't.

In sin and guilt I would wait out periods of time, in self-penance as if I was waiting for God to cool down. I hid, thinking that hiding was in some way humble or helpful. Like it would ease the pain of insufficiency, but it never did.

Because what hiding does do, what it's so effective at, is adding disconnection to shame. It won't remove the painful feelings, but it will cause us to live apart from God in it, and it's there that we begin to feed on disorder. A disorder that tears us from the union we truly thirst for. Because if we can't quench our thirst for healing and acceptance in Divine Love, we'll attempt to quench it somewhere else—food and alcohol, streaming, shopping, sex, pornography, anger, etc.

Ironically, not taking our shame to Love causes us to satisfy it ourselves in ways that often create more shame. All the while God sees us, He never turns away. He's there, standing at the door of our shame, knocking.

After a while, I realised this whole cycle of hiding, stewing in shame and disorder out of fear of facing it, only to face it eventually anyway with an even larger rap sheet of malfunction, was ridiculous. That God was intimately aware of my failures and that my waiting to run to Him in them was only causing unnecessary harm to our communion.

I began to shorten the hide time, little by little until eventually there was none. I began turning to God immediately after my disorder, and then amidst it. I began to unhide.

HEALTHY SHAME

Despite popular belief, shame is not all bad. The Merriam-Webster dictionary defines *shame* as "a painful emotion caused by consciousness of guilt, shortcoming, or impropriety."[82] We Christians would call that conviction, the natural consequence of living in a way that is harmful to us, to others, and to the communion we were created for. If we felt no shame for hitting a child, abusing someone, theft, or drunkenness, for example, we would consider it a sign of psychosis. Some healthy shame is a good thing, intended to draw us back to healing just as a broken bone draws us to the doctor.

There is, however, an unhealthy, toxic shame. The kind of shame which, instead of saying "I *failed*" makes the personal statement "I'm a *failure*." That instead of saying "I made a mistake" says, "I am a mistake." This is the demonic voice, the voice of death. It wants to make us despair for who we are, not just what we've done. Toxic shame makes us feel unworthy as a human being, causes depression, and separates us from God. Healthy shame turns us toward God. Toxic shame beckons us to hide.

The key to a liberating, intermingling life with God in the deep self is to discern between healthy and toxic shame, and to live a life of unhiding, experiencing God's divine love and mercy in the midst of it. It's to experience communion through our conscious experiences of insufficiency and sin, the life we were predestined for.

Scholars believe at the root of the English word *shame* is an old High German word that means "to cover."[83] Here, hidden away in our very language is the memory of that original moment when our shame caused us to place something between God and ourselves. When we first allowed it to break communion, when we first experienced unseenness. Naked living, living with Divine Love in our deep self, is our loving determination to come out of hiding, and to never cover ourselves again.

To live this way is at the very heart of repentance.

TURN YOUR EYES TO JESUS

My earliest conscious memory of fear or shame toward God was as an eight-year-old boy. Middle-class suburban life was proving unsatisfactory for me, so I turned to a life of crime. Convincing my younger cousin to join me, I founded a club, aptly named The Stealing Club, and started spending my spare hours pinching sour lollies and Hubba Bubba chewing gum from the dairy at the top of our street.

The rush was as addictive as the sugar, and soon enough we were hitting harder targets every week. The pinnacle of which was Nanna's jewellery box. The lollies we ate in the dense bush behind our house, but the jewellery we had no idea what to do with. So we buried it.

One day, bored of the usual routine and looking to up the ante, we elected to rob a supermarket on a routine shopping trip with Dad. We donned our fluro bum bags (fanny packs as they're called in the US) and filled them up with whatever easy grabs we could find.

A Cadbury Moro bar, a bag of rubber bands, more Hubba Bubba, and some black and white pegs.

Unfortunately for us, we were eight, and not subtle. The check-out lady saw us pocketing the goods, and whilst Dad was paying for his items and we were standing shiftily by the exit, she gave the game away. When we got to the car, he told us to empty our coffers. The gig was up, the high years of The Stealing Club came to its terrible end.

At home, Dad sent me immediately up the stairs to my bedroom with a single ominous command: "Go pray that God forgives you for what you've done." Knowing Dad, he would have been holding back the laughter as much as any anger. He probably said it with a smirk on his face, but to my eight-year-old ears, it sounded eternally consequential.

I ran upstairs to my bed, dropped to my knees, and prayed, "God, I know I made a mess of my life. If You'll only forgive me I promise I'll be better. I can turn this thing around!" I've never forgotten that feeling. It was my first authentic experience of repentance.

To many of us that's what repentance is, an apology. We do something wrong, say the magic word, and God is at best delighted, or at worst forced, to forgive us. It's transactional, like swiping our card to get a product. God may be angry with us but because of what His Son did on the cross we can twist His arm not to punish us. We see sin primarily as a legal issue, and prayer the place we go to settle our account. Though it's not wrong that God forgives us because of Christ's work of the cross, this gospel is painfully reductive.

When Adam and Eve sinned, they hid *before* they ever received any judgement. In their story we see that the first, and greatest, damage done by our sin is relational, not legal. That's not to say that our disorder doesn't have powerful implications for us, our relationships, and the world, only that all that illness stems from the disconnection with God it creates.

In severing our thirst from its Source, all attempts to quench it are disordered. In that sentiment, we discover a new dimension to what we mean when we say *repentance*.

The word used for "repentance" in the New Testament is *metanoia* and it contains two senses, "a change of mind" and "regret/remorse."[84] In the Old Testament the most common Hebrew word used is *sub*, which is typically translated as "turn" or "return." This turning is often thought of only in relation to our behaviour, which is true, but it's also true of something else, our seeing and being seen.

We're not only turning *away* from something in repentance, but *toward* Someone.

To turn our bodies is to also turn our eyes. It's very difficult to turn toward a new direction without a line of sight. When we turn from the disorder we're living in, it matters that we set our eyes not on right behaviour, or on fixing ourselves, but on the reconciling eyes of God. We don't turn toward moralism in repentance, we turn toward Divine Love.

It's very possible to ask for forgiveness and to live differently but, in our deep self, still live hiding from God. Our ethics change, but not our divine relating. When, in the midst of our repentance, we try to perform rather than reconcile, we whittle the whole experience down to transactionalism.

But if the first break is in relationship, not a law, then it's only in returning to full communion that we truly repent. Unhiding, then, involves not only an apology, not only a turning away from our disorder, but a turning back again to a mutual gaze with God in our Dark Ocean.

That can be difficult when we feel intense shame and guilt. It's easier to punish ourselves, refusing to be open to redeeming love, to avoid abiding prayer in the ensuing disconnection. But that's toxic shame speaking, the voice that tells us to hide rather than be restored.

Living repentance, not just visiting it, is about refusing toxic, hiding shame once and for all. It's to live in a continual state of emotional, mental, and spiritual nudity. It's relational, not transactional, holding its gaze with God in and through our failure and shame. Repentance of this kind is true humility because it lives acknowledging both the continued disorder of our condition and the unceasing reconciling thirst of God to be one with us regardless.

It doesn't diminish sin, because it actually grieves us more to know that it's relationship, not some law, that suffers most. What it does do, though, is diminish sin's power, its enticement to hiding, its desire for us to live in shame and not love.

True repentance involves turning toward God, to see Him and be seen *in* our feelings of shame and guilt, and to embrace spiritual nakedness. It's to live the liberation of knowing that God sees anyway, that He's full of loving kindness, mercy, and forgiveness, and that there's no reason to ever hide again. Even though it can be painful at times. It's to give up this to-and-fro process of sinning, hiding, confessing, and returning and to live a life of unbroken, continual transparency, humility, and openness with God.

It's a *yes* to feeling healthy shame and the pain of our mistakes, but it's a greater *yes* to being in God through it. Because the greater the experience of pain our living brings, the greater the experience of love and healing it brings with it. God is far greater than the pain we cause.

GOD IS NAKED TOO

Since the garden, despite God's continuous calls to front up to what's disordered within us and return to His love, we keep clothing ourselves with the leaves and branches of the world. Covering our minds, hearts, and lives in its fallen foliage. Something had to be done. Someone had to redeem nakedness. That someone was Christ.

The very way in which God overcomes our sin and restores us to the intimacy He created us for was through His own profound experience of shame. Only His wasn't for error, but in innocent outward-reaching desire. Rejected, hated, accused, and beaten, Jesus the very Word of God was publicly humiliated for His vulnerable self-offering. God made Himself available and we not only rejected Him, but publicly shamed Him for it.

Roman crucifixions at that time included the full stripping of its victims. It was intended to inflict ultimate embarrassment and humiliation on those it persecuted. So it's very likely that hanging on that cross, God Himself was naked. Arms nailed wide open, God

Himself unhid, taking the very nakedness that kept us from Him, using it to make us safe again. He made it holy.

Jesus took the full weight of our separation upon Himself, all its rejection, fear, anxiety, and darkness, and bore it in His being. He felt what it was like to want to hide, He felt our pain and stayed there, offering Himself in the midst of it. In doing so he showed us what it looks like to live the vulnerability, and risk, of baring all in love.

On the cross, God experienced shame so that shame could experience love. And it's there, in Jesus' staying with us in His most intense experience of shame, that we learn how to be the same. To stay naked, to allow ourselves to be seen in the very depth of us where our shame is most potent and to still look to God, is precisely what the cross is about. Christ sees us in and through shame and invites us to return the favour in a mutual, naked, gaze.

This is one dimension of "unceasing prayer" because in our nakedness we learn not to break communion even in our failure. And it's deeply transformative. Joshua Elzner, theologian and writer on prayer, explores the redemptive power of this mutual gaze, saying:

> Just as for God to speak is to do, and to look is to love, so for him to gaze is for him to transform, to bring radiance and beauty. Our very existence, our very beauty as a person, is the fruit of this sustained gaze of love. And yet there are certain gifts, a process of transformation, which can only occur when this gaze is fully accepted, when our eyes open to meet the eyes that look upon us.[85]

The very act of God's gazing upon us in love, Elzner tells us, transforms and beautifies us. And yet, only if we return it. Only if we simply don't turn away. When we add hiding to our shame, and refuse to live in nakedness with God, we say *no* to the flow of His loving, abiding, and forgiving, and to seeing Him entering our being.

Maybe this kind of unhidden soul is part of what Paul refers to as our "unveiled faces" when he says, "And we all, who with unveiled faces contemplate the Lord's glory, are being transformed into his image with ever-increasing glory, which comes from the Lord, who is the Spirit."[86] Maybe the unveiling of ourselves, and our refusing to hide, is precisely the place where beholding turns into loving transformation.

For that, all we need to do is stop, open our souls to God to be seen, and to share our shame, regret, and grief with His Spirit. It's not a rational, transactional experience, it's a "Dark Ocean intermingling of knowing love" kind. A seeing God from the ache of our deep.

Hiding in the bushes does nothing to heal or liberate our shame. Neither does pushing the feeling of guilt down to watch Netflix, trying to drink, exercise, sleep, or deny our way out of it. We employ all kinds of self-destructive behaviour in the bushes of our hearts to deal with what only Love can truly liberate.

In Genesis we read that when Adam and Eve hid, God came looking for them, calling out, "Where are you?"[87] God knew exactly where they were. His question wasn't for Him, it was for us. It was an invitation to give up pretending there's anywhere for us to hide. He asks not so He can shame or belittle us, but so we can be free.

While we stew in our mistakes, self-hatred, and toxic shame, the voice of the Spirit whispers, "Where are you?" the Son stands knocking on the door of our soul, the Prodigal Father runs toward us from far off, arms wide open.

In His Sermon on the Mount, Jesus taught, "If someone takes your coat, do not withhold your shirt from them."[88] I believe that's not only a physical invitation, but a spiritual one too. Yes, it's about sharing with those in need, but it can also be an invitation to a liberating way of living. To live a spirit of wild openness toward God. One that isn't worried about derobing our pride and giving up our need for performance and self-sufficiency.

A life lived poor in spirit, with a contrite heart and a deep openness to divine communion. A willingness to bare all rather than self-protect.

Why not spend a few minutes each day with God, taking off the tunics of shame, guilt, and self-preservation you use to cover your deep self. As if to say to God, "See, I've nothing to hide. All my failure, all my beauty, and everything in between is Yours. Only let me have You and Your presence always." You could even name the items you're taking off, the things you hate to admit, that you fear being exposed, and that live in the shadows of you, opening yourself to God.

Day by day practising this seeingness with God, allowing Him in to the places you'd otherwise avoid, you may find your reflexes toward hiding in future failure diminishing. You may notice God's compassion more, His quiet and forgiving love, and a greater absence of the pride within you that tries to prove and perform its way into His presence.

Spiritual nudity is one of the great heights of thirst-quenching, meeting our most deep desire for unconditional love. A love that is meaningless to us if it's not experienced, and experienced where it feels most needed.

Why not now, this moment, take a deep breath and open up your places of shame to God.

Come out of hiding, allow His loving eyes to see you.

Reveal your whole self, experience His love.

And never turn away again.

Chapter 11

Letting

"God of the deep places,
I'm relying on You now to do Your work
in the unlanguageable caverns of my soul."
Prayer Vol. 02

If we keep saying *yes* to Love, we'll find ourselves arriving at a place where we're no longer able to offer anything to Him in return in the progress of our intimacy. Beyond bringing our bodies into alignment with our truest Christ desires, beyond opening ourselves up and giving Him consent to our aches, pains, and shame, we will arrive to a place of *letting*. Here we're fully at the mercy of God's will, His timing and desire for us in our uniqueness.

In letting we relent ultimate control of our communion to God.

The deepest places of prayer are like this, utterly beyond us. I think that's what Paul is hinting at in Romans when he says, "We do not know what we ought to pray for, but the Spirit himself intercedes for us through wordless groans."[89] Paul traveled to the third heaven, was taught the gospel by Christ Himself, raised the dead, and saw mysteries he couldn't speak of. But despite all that, Paul knew there was prayer taking place in him that he knew nothing about. Deep within, prayer happened to him as much as he did it.

Prayer is far greater than us, and the shape our individual communion takes, after all of our bringing ourselves to it, is beyond us. It's a work of grace. So eventually, we all need to experience the free fall of throwing ourselves wholly into the trust that, despite what we see or feel, God is doing His good work. We have to embrace a loving, faithful blindness.

Faith like this can sound more romantic than it is. In reality, it's painful, offensive, and goes against every reflex of self-preservation we have within us. We love being in control or, in the very least, in the know. Because understanding is its own form of control. It removes the need for faith and radical trust. That kind of control feels empowering, makes us feel secure, and gives us a sense that our lives are going where we want them to go.

But the problem, as we've seen, is that we hardly know what we thirst for or at least the true magnitude of it. Our Dark Ocean is full of counter-currents and untouched depths that require the Spirit of wisdom and love to plunge and transform. If the activity of the Spirit is restricted to only what we can conceive then we live chained to our own self-awareness. If, on the other hand, we can learn to let go, even of our ability to see and know the work God is doing in us, then He can draw us into miraculous spaces.

I see my life as a long string of happy accidents. At high school in my metal-music days I made a pact with my atheist friends never to play Christian music. I even made them sign a written contract saying if they ever saw me singing Christian songs on an acoustic guitar in church, or anywhere for that matter, they had permission to end me on the spot.

Nothing was lower than Christian music. Especially acoustic Christian music. Only six years later that's exactly what I was doing. And loving it.

When I did play that kind of music, my dream became to lead prophetic worship sets at events full of charismatically inspired prayer. I imagined hours-long sets of spontaneous songs inspiring masses to prayer, intercession, and spiritual experience. But when I picked up a guitar and sang, out came old psalmic folk songs about pain and hope. I found myself not in conferences and prophetic worship nights but living rooms, bars, and the highways and byways of our generation in a time when the millennial exodus from the church was fast growing.

It wasn't my idea, but it was again an incredible gift.

Later, chronic illness would bring all that to an end, and in the ashes of a music vocation I thought would see me through to the grave, a ministry in prayer bubbled up. Not the kinds of charismatic prayer that had been my DNA but the quiet, gentle, vulnerable kind that often spoke not to the bold and confident but the poor in spirit.

I'd spent my twenties in intercessory prayer groups, worship nights, and interpersonal prayer meetings. My origin story in prayer is thoroughly charismatic. But when the calling came to dialogue in prayer with others, it was while I was in the middle of a profound spiritual transformation my illness had brought about (a story I share fully in my book *Beholding*).

In the end it wasn't strong, energising prayer I was called to share despite my firm love and experience of it. It was weakness, dependence, and the beauty that comes from a poverty of spirit. Instead of charismatic declarations from the stages of church communities on Sundays, I found myself writing quiet poetry, devotional reflections on God's work in the soul, retreats, and a sort of contemplative-charismatic resourcing of anyone who was thirsty.

All of that was, and is, a gift. It just wasn't what I had planned for a spiritual or working life. Since that summer God spoke to me, saying, "Come home to Me, son," and Katie's and my turning toward God and His kingdom, I've longed for an active, charismatic life. I had friends then, and still do now, who travel to needing countries to pray for the sick and who see genuine physical and profoundly miraculous healings.

I have other friends who go from place to place, preaching and sharing dreams and visions they've had, encouraging and strengthening the church, helping to steer her ever deeper into God's loving heart. I know still others who, when doing street ministry, see the most incredible homecomings from truly broken people and others who really did take up my dream to lead energising and beautiful worship nights in their communities.

All those years ago, when I spent nights crying on the floor asking to know and experience God, all of *that* is what I imagined. But that hasn't been the work of my life. That hasn't been the communion I've experienced. For a while I thought it was because I was doing something wrong. Now I see that it was the Spirit who was taking me on a different, surprising, and deeply fulfilling journey.

Instead of an active, traveling life God led me into retreat and reflection. He withdrew me further and further from the confident, vital other-ministry I was used to and into excruciating solitude, quiet, and emptiness. There God began to give me a language for the soul, and a writer's touch. In the quiet He taught me about this intermingling life.

Later, I would see the harmony between what I was experiencing and the teaching of the monastics. I'd find my experience in their spirituality and teaching. But until I discovered myself in the wider history of the church, I thought I was losing it. Like I was failing somehow.

The more I let the Spirit lead, the less I knew where I was going. I was loving the growing union I was experiencing, but it came with an undeniable sense of uncertainty. Letting God through those years was about paying attention to what God was doing, and not fixating on what He wasn't. It meant not comparing life and communion to my idea of what it should be like, and being free to accept His.

I had to trust that what God was doing in me was good, that it was a work of love, that I was being cared for and transformed into the me He made me to be rather than being left behind. In my blindness to His work, I had to say yes. I had to give up control not only of my life, but of my deep self.

And I've had to do that plenty. Because additional to the things God does in my vocational life, is the mystery of His timing with my inner healing, anxieties, the meeting of my deep desires, and the transformation I so desperately long for. God could heal it all in a moment, but He doesn't. He cherishes my trust, and does the much needed work I'd rather shortcut.

When I did surrender to God in those years, it bore real fruit in my life. I began to write, a ministry in prayer was born, others who suffered illness and loss found God in my aching and longing prayers. In seasons where I fought it, I only experienced disappointment and sadness.

The prayer God was longing to grow in and share through me, it seemed, was the full opening up of my deep self to His love. To unhiding, to opening up and being loved, to adoring and valuing God for who He is and making His presence paramount in the midst of my brokenness. All other prayer is important, but for a life of divine intimacy, this is foundational. That six- or seven-year journey of disorientation taught me that, but it required a huge amount of acceptance and trust.

In all this time, the work the Spirit has done in and through me has consistently surprised me. I find myself where I am, and who I am, not because of any plan or intelligence, or even a vision of what a prayerful life should be, but because God helped me come to the realisation that it's better when I don't follow my own plans for my life, or for my healing. I'm better when I'm not trying to be who I think I should be, but who God is making me.

When I move past making sense of God's deep work in me and simply consent.

When I let God garden me.

CHRIST THE GARDENER

Our first encounter with the resurrected Christ happens in the gospel of John between Him and Mary Magdalene. It's a surprising moment. Jesus has just conquered death, overcome shame, sin, and the powers of darkness and of this world. Mary, one of His disciples, has just seen two angels in the tomb where His body should be.

Those of us reading with the mind of the world are now likely expecting to encounter this risen Victor in all pomp and glory, riding on golden chariots, wielding heavenly flames of divine justice, proceeding into creation with multitudes of angels. But that's not what we find. Instead, we read this:

> Now Mary stood outside the tomb crying. As she wept, she bent over to look into the tomb and saw two angels in white, seated where Jesus' body had been, one at the head and the other at the foot.
>
> They asked her, "Woman, why are you crying?"
>
> "They have taken my Lord away," she said, "and I don't know where they have put him." At this, she turned round and saw Jesus standing there, but she did not realise that it was Jesus.

He asked her, "Woman, why are you crying?
Who is it you are looking for?"

Thinking he was the gardener, she said, "Sir, if
you have carried him away, tell me where you have
put him, and I will get him."

Jesus said to her, "Mary."

She turned towards him and cried out in
Aramaic, "Rabboni!" (which means "Teacher").[90]

Jesus, living God, ruler of the cosmos, is mistaken for a
Gardener.

Scholars agree that this is no mistake. John's gospel is full of
allusions to creation and re-creation. The opening line, "In the
beginning was the Word," is an invitation to see Christ present
at the very beginning of creation and to hint at a new beginning.
Later, when accounting for Jesus' crucifixion and resurrection,
John reminds us of this cosmic arc, saying, "At the place where
Jesus was crucified, there was a garden, and in the garden a new
tomb, in which no one had ever been laid."[91]

Why does it matter so much to John that we keep remember-
ing these things happened in gardens? Because that's our place of
greatest failure and vulnerability. Because it's in the garden where
we first felt shameful, in the garden where we first hid, and in the
garden, we failed our commission to cultivate the earth and our
own souls and so it's to the garden Jesus appears to heal us.

As seventeenth-century preacher Isaac Ambrose puts it:

Because a garden was the place wherein we fell,
and therefore Christ made choice of a garden
to begin there the greatest work of our redemption: in the first garden was the beginning of all
evils; and in this garden was the beginning of our
restitution from all evils; in the first garden, the
first Adam was overthrown by Satan, and in this
garden the second Adam overcame, and Satan
himself was by him overcome.[92]

Gardens play a significant role not only in our vocation and
fall, but our redemption too. But there's more to this image, there's
something personal happening.

Because only a few chapters earlier in his gospel John recounts
Jesus' words, "I am the vine; you are the branches. If you remain
in me and I in you, you will bear much fruit."[93] Jesus expresses
our *in*ness with Him through the image of agriculture. The garden, then, isn't only an image of the grand story of creation, fall,
redemption, but of what it means to live in God Himself. To that
end, Jesus even calls His Father "the gardener," and we the vines
He cares for.[94]

The garden imagery isn't only about the cosmos and the salvation of the world, it's about our very souls. John seems to want us
to see the risen Christ first and foremost as a humble gardener of
souls. I love the way Charles Spurgeon, nineteenth-century Baptist
pastor and poet-preacher, puts it:

Behold, the church is Christ's Eden, watered by
the river of life, and so fertilized that all manner
of fruits are brought forth unto God; and he, our
second Adam, walks in this spiritual Eden to dress
it and to keep it; and so by a type we see that we are
right in "supposing him to be the gardener." Thus
also Solomon thought of him when he described
the royal Bridegroom as going down with his
spouse to the garden when the flowers appeared on
the earth and the fig tree had put forth her green
figs; he went out with his beloved for the reserva-
tion of the gardens.[95]

Spurgeon makes the connection not only of Christ walking the
garden of our souls like God walked among the flora of Eden, but
of Christ as the bridegroom described by Solomon in the Song of
Songs. For him, we are the field of flowers and fruit, springing up
and beautified by Christ in which He longs to dwell and enjoy.

In the garden we tried to satisfy our thirst ourselves and became
enslaved to it as a result. In the new garden God satiates His thirst
for our souls by coming to us, walking amidst our disorder, liberating us from our hiding.

That's a lot of imagery and theology, I know, but what it has
to say for our souls is profound. We are no longer left to our own
devices to cultivate this intermingling life with God. Sure, we do our
part, this *is* a relationship. But the deepest work is His. We now live
at the mercy of the tender Gardener who is unafraid to reach into

the soil of our being, to take what's rotten within us to fertilise a new heart of love and intimacy.

Just as He promised He would in Ezekiel, the Divine Spouse is beautifying us. Pruning back the wild edges formed in us by a broken world and our disordered living so He may dwell ever more freely in our deep self.

And yet, this process of letting God do the work in us, of simply abiding and allowing Him to make us fruitful, feels utterly unnatural.

END PRODUCTIVITY, ENTER FRUITFULNESS

We citizens of the twenty-first century walk with a cultural limp when it comes to our letting God. That limp is the mortal wound inflicted on our psyche by the Industrial Revolution. To be sure the Industrial Revolution brought with it untold benefits, not the least of which was raising millions out of poverty. It's generated access, technology, and opportunity unprecedented in human history.

But there's also been an unexpected side effect that has deeply affected us in this area of *letting*, and that's the obsession it has created in us for individual productivity.

Before the Industrial Revolution, people were the ones who made our tables, clothes, machinery, and materials. That meant the generation of goods and services moved at a human pace. People can only be awake so many hours, work for so long without growing tired, and store all their knowledge and skills in their own minds and bodies. Nations rose, fell, and plateaued on the number of how many hands they had to work.

But all of that changed with the creation of urban factory lines and powerful machinery that could either replace or streamline human work. Machinery increased the pace of our production. Where the pace of life was once set by limitations naturally endowed on humans by our Creator, it soon came to be dictated to us by the power of the industrial engine.

Efficient factories churning out masses of products became the norm. No more slowly waiting for food to grow or carpenters to build tables, machines now helped make them without sweat, and new trains, planes, and steamships meant they could be farmed out to the public at a rapid pace.

With electricity also becoming more widely available, we could work through the night under luminous lights, further increasing productivity. By the mid-1900s the invention of things like the microwave, washing machine, and dishwasher promised a world where we could do more than we ever could before with less work. The later invention of the internet and global interconnection put that process into hyperdrive.

And all this shaped us. We've largely forgotten the natural rhythms of creation, how slow-food is grown, and what a previously normal expectation of a day's work for a human could be. That's a problem for our understanding of what Jesus is talking about when He speaks of us as vines, living from the branch of His presence.

Because vines, branches, and gardens don't operate on productivity. They live by the rule of fruitfulness. They're not in control, they're at the mercy of the sun, moon, and wind. Vines don't produce fruit all year round at a steady pace, they're pruned and shaped. Death and waiting are a natural part of their fruiting year on year.

Where productivity is about human control, fruitfulness is about dependency. And its fruitfulness, not productivity, that is the primary criterion of love and spiritual growth in the New Testament. The most articulate pronouncement of that truth being Jesus' own words in John 15:5, "I am the vine; you are the branches. If you remain in me and I in you, you will bear much fruit; apart from me you can do nothing."

We are not factory lines pumping out prayer, character, and work. We're branches, bringing only out of ourselves the love, joy, peace, and vitality that are first experienced in the Vine. This is why what we in modern times would prefer to call "products" of the Spirit are instead called "fruit" by the apostle Paul in Galatians 5.

Think of the process of any fruiting tree. First, it's a tiny seed planted in soil. From its earliest stage that seed is utterly dependent on the richness of the soil for its survival. There, it lives in darkness, hidden deep enough from the world to be kept from predators and strong winds, close enough to the surface to receive rain and grow its sprouts.

Soon, a seed becomes that small sprout, then a trunk. Finally, after years of rain, weather, and soil-dependent growth, it adds to its trunk branches that begin to leaf. By the time the tree finally does produce fruit, its first harvests don't even produce the best. It fruits, sheds its leaves, is pruned, then fruits again. That process continues year on year, often not producing its best work until years later in its life.

That's what communion is like. It couldn't be further from a factory if it tried. And how freeing that is!

Because you and I will experience plenty of seasons where we see no fruit on the tree. Where it feels like all we're seeing are branches falling to the ground around us, only death. We may notice seeds from last season's harvest falling into the soil of our lives, but as sure as we see them drop, they're covered again, hidden for years to come.

Last year we had such a deep sense of God's presence, this year we can't sense Him anywhere. Maybe it's the loss of something, ongoing illness, crippling anxiety or depression or life circumstances we can't change or control. We pray and seek God earnestly to free or heal us but it persists. Maybe it's that we long to love Him more than we do, we ache for it, but our hearts are dim and our flame just a flicker.

The image of God as Gardener means we can trust Him in and through all these seasons, regardless of what we can see. It means we can relent to His pruning, His watering, *and* His fruiting His love and intimacy with us and through us. If God is a gardener, then in every season we can let Him, rest in His presence, and keep saying *yes*. We don't have to understand, we don't have to feel or even see it, we can simply trust. And when we do fruit and our lives leap into spring, we can thank Him for bearing in us what can only be produced by His loving kindness.

This kind of spirituality doesn't always show up in our calendar looking very "productive," as we define it. It's difficult to quantify beholding God when our lives look far more like winter than spring.

But if Jesus is to be trusted, it's the only way to live what we may otherwise define as a productive life today. That's the miracle of Love. In rest we find the power for action, in receiving love we're awakened to a love for others, in being the garden we're shaped into beauty, fruitfulness, and shade for the world in which we live.

We may be able to modify our behaviour, but only the Spirit can transform us. For that, we need a Gardener.

Recently, for a season I decided to pray a dangerous prayer, I asked God to show me how much He loved me. I was hoping for a mystical experience, a vision, or anything really that could surge me on in devotion and affection for Him. I got my answer, but not how I'd hoped.

What I experienced was a sudden and profound awareness of the lack of *my* love! Day after day, hour after hour, it was as if I noticed every erring thought, every preference for the world over His presence, and the perpetual unlitness of my heart. It was painful. I knew that I wanted to love God more, but now I was seeing just how much more. This wasn't a mystical experience at all, this felt like cruelty.

Then quietly, in the middle of my spiritual grief, a new appreciation and awareness of God's love began growing. I wasn't having a "filling" experience, but my "emptying" experience brought God's love into much sharper focus. The chasm between our loves was vast, and yet He continued to love me without reserve and with vital, vulnerable longing. God was giving far more than He was getting, and yet He kept pouring it out.

To make matters worse, seeing my deficit, and God's audacious love, didn't change the fact that I couldn't do anything about it. Like the sun rising all I could do was be still and receive as the powerful warmth of His compassionate and selfless love poured over me wave after wave. I wanted desperately to offer something more in return, but no matter how hard I tried I remained little. I was simply a recipient, and He wanted me to know that.

For weeks I was gripped with simultaneous grief and liberating joy. Oscillating between trying to offer more and giving up when I couldn't. I was astounded by how little He needed. I'd hoped for an experience that could help me love God more, instead He sat me down and showed me that it wouldn't change anything if I could. That in reality, there is no amount of love a human heart can conjure that could equal what is effortless for Him to be.

In reality, I can only love Him with who He is. I can only love Him with Him.

When John wrote one of the latest letters to the early church, he seemed to want to remind them of the same thing, "We love, because He first loved us."[96] That's what it means to receive God as Gardener, to let God be the origin and fulfilment of our transformation into love. The truth is, we just can't love Him enough. Any love we can give Him springs not from ourselves and our own strength, but from the very love we've received from Him in the first place. That's how the fruit of the Spirit works.

We don't change ultimately via willpower and discipline or through knowledge and information, but by opening ourselves up persistently to love, that the Spirit may rush in and garden our souls with the vital love of our Beloved. In our truest sense, we are little more than soil crying out for rain. Our knowing and experiencing God is His beginning to end. All we can do is love Him with what we have, be it little or large, and thank Him for that.

We're safe opening our souls' deepest longings to God, because He longs to satisfy them more than we do. As Madame Guyon tells us, "God desires to give the divine heart more than we wish to possess it." We may rightly fear that level of vulnerability with anyone else on earth, but with God, we're safe. We are His garden, and He loves us.

That doesn't mean we don't play our part. Ours is to keep saying *yes*, to bring our minds and bodies into our new true identity as Beloved, to remind ourselves of the magnitude of this story, to quench our thirst in heaven. But it does mean that ultimately we relinquish control of the deepest work, living as fertile soil for the tender hands of the Gardener.

To His turning, sowing, and pruning, we say *yes*. To our winters and our springs, we say *yes*. To our darknesses and storms, we say *yes*. To the watering of the rains, we say *yes*. To our awakening, flourishing, and beautifying, we say *yes*.

Eternal Waters

Chapter 12

Consummation

"My awaiting Your arrival,
is in so many ways, Your arrival."

Prayer Vol. 02

Sitting in our spa one evening, underneath the gem-lit canopy of a clear night sky, a calmness came over me. I'd been anxious that day about usual life things—work, health, family, direction—and had come out here after our boys were asleep to let the sediment of it all sink down in the heat of the water. I felt empty spiritually but I wanted time with One I knew was worth more than my worrying.

Looking up at the stars, I could see the Milky Way with incredible clarity. The waves of the beach nearby, a gentle roar reminding me of the persistence of life, water comes in, water recedes, water always is. Awake to the moment, a stillness came over me and I closed my eyes.

What happened next is difficult to explain. I've seen pictures before in prayer, and had experiences of God's love amidst them, but this was something else. I felt God showing me Himself as trinity. In an instant I felt thoroughly caught up in God, immersed in His love and the Conversation. I saw, but didn't see, an image of God in this way. Like trying to remember a face from a dream in the morning the experience felt like being part of the rushing waters of God in God.

It was personal, loving, volcanic, yet silent and unthreatening. It felt as though my whole body was going to explode whilst simultaneously melting into perfect peace.

It lasted, I'm sure, no more than a few seconds, then it left me. By the time the vision diminished, I was aware of my surroundings again. I opened my eyes and saw, right above me in my line of sight, a long-tailed meteor tracing the skyline from left to right, lighting up the atmosphere around it.

A divine wink.

Heaven had pierced my existence for just a moment, my soul caught up into something profoundly other. I wanted to stay there, I wanted to live there, but I couldn't.

And that's just the reality of this age, we drink, but not as we one day will.

In this life, heaven punctuates.

In the next, it will be permanent reality.

Our journey ends where it doesn't end, in the living anticipation of that incredible moment when all disorder is done away, death departs, and we're fully given over to the Love we've spent our entire lives pining for. The moment of our final consummation.

Then heaven and earth will be reborn into each other and we ourselves will be finally transformed into what we were always made to be. There will be no division between our deep thirst for Love and our thinking and loving. No more fighting against ourselves to receive God's love and live in harmony with Him. Our souls will be collected into one, in Christ, and we will never spend another moment apart.

The war of desires will be over, won by the Yearning for every person who wants Him. No more inner doors, no more hiding, just wide-open transparency and freedom.

But even then, our thirst won't end, it will simply be transformed. Because it's part of our image, the imprint of God, not of the fall. Desire is who we are. What we experience then won't be the ceasing of thirst, but the perpetual and unhindered filling of it by God Himself. There, by grace, we will experience God as He has experienced Himself for eternity. His vital, other-yearning, and unfettered presence.

It will be like drinking wine all day without ever getting drunk, the first cuddle with a newborn child, the height of sexual intimacy, the joy of celebrating with a friend, the rush of crossing the finish line first, and the jubilation of seeing the lost found, the sick healed, or the hungry filled.

But in perpetuity.

All of it experienced deep in the very foundation of our being. Permanent, constant, eternal.

We will thirst eternally, but be satisfied unceasingly in every moment. It will be the consummation of Christ's promise of our being caught up in Trinity, knowing what it's like to need in perfect security and without fear. We'll experience for the first time ever what it's like to desire without insecurity, to drink the Spirit without pause.

Can you imagine it? Take your greatest experience of pleasure in this life, multiply it by eternity, and increase the intensity a millionfold, and you'll still not even be close to what eternal life will be. It will live inside you, more permanent than breathing. More sure than your very consciousness.

This matters, because as extravagant as the gift of our intermingling, our union with God, is in this life, it is still only a *taste*. There's a "now and not yet" element not only to the kingdom, but to this co-experience of God in our souls. Paul calls the beauty of that experience in this life "a *deposit* guaranteeing our inheritance until the redemption of those who are God's possession."[97]

That astounds me. Because in my life I've felt incredible joy, peace, love, kindness, and compassion in the Spirit. I've seen God move powerfully through prayer, I've witnessed lives transformed, experienced dreams and visions, and had transcendent moments in the stillness of prayer and yet all of that is the entrée. A gift to whet my appetite in the dry wilderness of this world in anticipation of the abundant feast of eternal life.

Let that sink in, and simmer.

Where we're heading is unfathomably good.

It's worth the thirsting and the yearning.

We *will* be finally satisfied.

We need to remember all this when the pain of our thirst is acute. When we feel discouraged about how we feel with God, when the war on our disorder feels like a battle we can no longer fight. In those moments, when it feels too much, we won't find our strength within or around us, but through the prophetic vision of *this* incoming life.

This world is in some ways a fast, yes, but for a feast to come.

This is a gospel for the addicted, the depressed, and the parent of a dying child, for the weak-willed, the single and weary justice worker, for the chronically sick, the spiritually lonely, and those for whom the reality of their life falls painfully short of expectations. This gospel is an *amen* to all longing. It beckons us to wait, to hold on, and to trust Him. To believe that His yearning love is more powerful than all this brokenness and that it's worth our lives to anticipate it.

This expectation-reality gap for what union with God in this life should feel like is something I wish I'd grasped more as a younger man. For a long time I grew tired of waiting for God to take the ache for Him away. It was insinuated in the communities I'd been part of that salvation or knowing God was meant to take it all away, that it was meant to satisfy me wholly, now. Seeking Him when that wasn't true for so long began to feel too costly. As did hope.

Day after day it just never felt like I had enough of Him, like the gospel just never quite finished what it began in my soul. No one told me that that was the spiritual life this side of eternity. No one told me that the presence of my thirst was the very presence of God, calling me deeper into Him.

If I'd known that, I may not have given up when I did. Not my faith, I never did again after that summer. What I mean is the fervent seeking of my earlier faith life, the anticipation of more. Can't that happen to us? We begin praying for God to do amazing things and believing Him for them, but over time, as we see only some prayers answered, as we have only a limited experience of Him, we diminish our expectations.

Thirsting feels too costly, too much, and so we bring the dial down a little.

I wish that in that season of my own, an older, wiser, loving pilgrim on this journey had sat with me and told me that all that disappointment was holy. That the presence of lack was the presence of eternity shining through. That in this life, answered prayer, experiences of God, justice, and drinking the Spirit are only a *deposit* and that's okay. That I should look to the end, that I should never forget it, that I should live backwards from there.

I may not have lost heart, I may not have seen my thirst as a problem.

Thankfully, those years were short lived and I rediscovered my holy longing. I took up the ache again and let it draw me deeper into, not further from, the Yearning. Only a few mornings ago I woke up weeping, crying for the Holy Spirit. The grief consumed me out of nowhere, this thirst to have more of what I already have. To offer a greater *yes*.

But it also invigorated me because I've come to know that aching as the very groan of the Spirit I'm longing for. My participating in the Conversation. God's longing for me from within me. His thirsting to be thirsted for. Now when I feel that way, I lean in, trusting that the thirst is His presence. That my thirsting is my drinking.

That's living in the ache of our thirst. That's what it means to embrace it as a gift rather than let it drive us into discouragement. It's to, in the words of Christopher West, become the *mystic*, someone who doesn't hide from the pain of desire but experiences God through it. It's to allow our pain, shame, and vulnerability to be a holy invitation for belovedness and not to numb it in the hope of relief.

It's to be *seen* by God.

Ultimately, that's where all this leads, to perfect seenness. The apostle John, whom theologians aptly name the "apostle of love," encourages, "Beloved, we are God's children now, and what we will be has not yet appeared; but we know that when he appears we shall be like him, because we shall see him as he is."[98] What is our final hope? That in the end our deep self will be fully beheld and will finally, without barrier or blindness, fully behold God as He is.

It is to an eternity of unbroken eye contact.

An everlasting nakedness with Love.

It's amazing to me that the mechanism for our final transformation isn't something transactional, a zapping of the Spirit, the signing of a covenant, or even a word spoken, but is instead a mutual gaze of love. What sets us free is being seen, and the more seen we are, the more we become who we were created to be. The more we become like God. Here, in the end, we discover that this learning to unhide in our souls isn't a fringe narrative but the very heartbeat of our story.

So why not behold God, look to Him, turn all your ache and desire toward His goodness and let Him have it? "Taste and see that the LORD is good,"[99] and see if He doesn't offer you Himself in place of whatever you thought you needed. Give Him your loneliness, your doubt, ambition, your want for sex and lust, your anxieties and fears. Tell Him that beneath all of that your true want is Him. Ask Him to be the end of that pain, to consummate it with His love and presence. Tell Him you want Him more.

Then, wait on Him.

Let Him arrive to you like He has to me in my illness, in my lostness, fear, and anxiety. Let Him replace your endless scrolling, your numbing with food and alcohol, your giving away your heart and body to others. Pray your pain. Simply sit in it together in silence, allowing Him to be with you there. Let Him be what He promises to be, living waters that satisfy the very seat of you.

Consecrate your heart, give it to Him. Set your body and mind aside for this "one thing," that in channelling up all this *dis*-ease within you it would welcome the presence of God and transform your very self.

Don't take your soul for granted. It's been welcomed into God Himself, marked with love, soaked in His presence. It is the most holy thing on earth now, the new tabernacle. Don't let the world into it, don't let it drink of anything else. Bring it into the Truth, what it deeply wants. Let your soul bring it to its Love.

My prayer is that you will be captivated by *this* gospel and that you might awaken to the magnitude and hope of a life lived quenching your thirst in Love. Yes, we anticipate its full finishing, but we can make the most of this deposit of ceaseless love today, this very moment. We can live a vital, life-giving intimacy with the Lover of heaven now, if we will only let Him in to do the work of love in our deep places.

Today, God is longing and knocking.

Yearning that you would only say *yes*.

Friend, may you say *yes*.

Gratitude

I set out here to write a book expressing a deep, inner journey that has taken me nearly two decades to articulate. I'd imagined that with it being so close to my heart, and such a vital part of this recent season for me, it would flow naturally and effortlessly. Instead, I found myself wrestling with God as He, once again, invited me to live in new depths the gospel I preach.

Sometimes, God's grace is experienced in a lightness and fluidity. At others, grace is the gift of a great struggle, drawing us into personal poverty so that God can be all the more God to us. Despite the subject of this book being the sweetness of God's divine love, my experience in writing it has very much been the latter.

Suffice to say, I am filled with gratitude for the patient people around me who assured me God was in this, and kept turning me back toward the faithfulness of my Beloved from whose eternal heart it sprang.

To Katie, you never flinched. When I was at my lowest with it, you reminded me of God's faithfulness time and again. You listened, you read heady drafts, you were a quiet presence when the pressure was intense and I couldn't see my way through it. Thank you for believing in this with me, and for being my own beloved.

To Mark Donovan, much of this final manuscript is shaped by your encouragement, loving critique, and thoughtful questions. You read almost five versions of a single chapter in a month, that's gold-medal worthy. I will forever be grateful for the friends in Christ you, Kelly, and your children are to us. Get some rest, will you, I'm starting a new script soon ...

Thank you also to Trish Rollo, who read the early manuscript and encouraged me along the way, as well as my many other friends who read and shared their personal encouragements with me and their endorsements at the front of this book.

I've never worked with another publisher before, but I find it hard to imagine I would meet a better friend and cheerleader anywhere in the world like my publisher Michael Covington. You really earned your keep on this one, my friend, encouraging me in the heart and vision of this book when I'd lost sight, keeping me on track, dealing with last-minute edits, and helping me trust that what is in my heart is truly communicated on these pages. Thank you. I'm grateful to work with someone who wholeheartedly gets me and what I'm called to. You really are a brother.

Likewise, to Stephanie, thank you for reminding me of the pastoral heart of this work and for your incredible eye to helping words and ideas flow. You're an encourager, I'm grateful you're on my team. Thank you also to Jack for your skill (and patience!) with my abundance of last-minute edits.

To the rest of the DCC team—James and the design team, Angie, Rudy, and everyone in marketing, I'm grateful that you've cared for the details and sharing of this book as much as I have.

Thank you also to Andrea Heinecke, my agent at Bindery, for your support and for helping me to continue to explore and grow in my surprising, newfound vocation as a writer.

I've become totally convinced that one couldn't hope to travel this road without the help of a loving, listening guide—mine over these years has been my spiritual director, Eamon Butler. Eamon, our conversations have held crucial space in these very mystical few years of mine. You've sat at the well with me, helped me touch my thirst, helped me to remain in my Beloved. Thank you.

In recent years I've felt the real weight and presence of those who have gone before me. For the many saints and mystics who helped me find a more expansive language for my deep self. This book is deeply inspired by Saint John, Augustine, Teresa of Ávila, John of the Cross, Madame Guyon, Joshua Elzner, and too many other great pray-ers to name.

For the monasteries, the ascetics, the desert dwellers, and the modern-day firebrands, you have been my great cloud of spiritual directors, a home for me, a vision for what's possible. I cannot thank you enough.

Finally, to you, reader, I'm grateful for your openness to this story. May it offer a small doorway to the rich and beautiful history of prayer that has marked the church since her earliest times.

Arohanui,

Strahan

Notes

1. Romans 8:26.

2. Hebrews 12:1.

3. Søren Kierkegaard, *Purity of Heart Is to Will One Thing: Spiritual Preparation for the Office of Confession*, trans. Douglas V. Steere (New York: Harper & Row, 1948).

4. Ronald Rolheiser, *The Holy Longing: The Search for a Christian Spirituality* (New York: Image, 2014), 3.

5. John 7:37 ESV.

6. Romans 7:15.

7. Genesis 2:18 NLV.

8. Psalms 42:2; 63:1 ESV.

9. Matthew 5:6.

10. Ronald Rolheiser speaks of the saintliness of desire and its space in Christian spirituality beautifully in his book *The Holy Longing: The Search for a Christian Spirituality* (New York: Image, 2014), 3.

11. Saint Augustine, *The Confessions.*

12. Genesis 4:7.

13. Credit to John Mark Comer for the *Frozen* observation in his book *Live No Lies: Recognize and Resist the Three Enemies That Sabotage Your Peace* (Colorado Springs: WaterBrook, 2021), 136.

14. Jeremy Lent, *The Patterning Instinct: A Cultural History of Humanity's Search for Meaning* (Amherst, NY: Prometheus Books, 2017), 380.

15. Mark Krupnik, "There's Active Drugs in Our Drinking Water: What's Being Done?" *Forbes*, July 19, 2022, www.forbes.com/ sites/forbestechcouncil/2022/07/19/theres-active-drugs-in-our-drinking-water-whats-being-done/?sh=11273be9753a.

16. Anna Lembke, *Dopamine Nation: Finding Balance in the Age of Indulgence* (New York: Dutton, 2021), 57.

17. Matthew 16:24.

18. Saint Augustine, *Enarrationes in Psalmos*, 37.14, emphasis mine.

19. Christopher West, *Fill These Hearts: God, Sex, and the Universal Longing* (New York: Image, 2013), 125.

20. Peter John Cameron, *Magnificat*, December 2001, 2–3.

21. I recorded a podcast about Ephesians 2:10 and being God's poem, you can listen here: https://open.spotify.com/episode/76aC TFTqCVYHvAtRUG7uo3?si=6941bcd04c4a4f23.

22. *Saint Augustine: Gospel of John* in *Nicene and Post-Nicene Fathers*, vol. 7, ed. Philip Schaff (New York: Cosimo Classics, 2007), 102.

23. Genesis 1:26 ESV.

24. Mother Teresa, "Co-Workers," Missionaries of Charity, accessed April 10, 2024, www.missionariesofcharity.org/sick _suffering_co_workers_readmore.html.

25. "Excerpts from the 'Varanasi Letter' Written by Mother Teresa in March 1993," Saint Max Church, accessed April 10, 2024, https://saint-max.org/Portals/0/Files/Parish/IThirst/Varanasi%20 Letter.pdf?ver=2020-09-01-102933-867.

26. Revelation 22:17 ESV.

27. ESV.

28. Isaiah 54:5; 62:5.

29. Hosea 2:19 ESV; 2:16.

30. Isaiah 57:7 NLT.

31. James 4:4.

32. Ezekiel 16:8–14.

33. Ephesians 5:31–32.

34. "'Varanasi Letter' Written by Mother Teresa," accessed April 10, 2024, https://saint-max.org/Portals/0/Files/Parish/IThirst/Varanasi%20Letter.pdf?ver=2020-09-01-102933-867.

35. Genesis 2:18 NLV.

36. John 19:28 ESV.

37. John 14:20.

38. Origen, *Homilies on Leviticus* 5.2, ed. W. A. Baehrens, *Die Griechischen Christlichen Schriftsteller*, vol. 29 (Leipzig, 1920), 336.

39. Psalm 139:12 ESV.

40. Psalms 43:5; 103:2 NET.

41. 1 Corinthians 3:16–17; 2 Corinthians 6:14–18; Ephesians 5:30–32.

42. "What Does the Word 'Logos' Mean?" Word by Word, accessed April 11, 2024, www.logos.com/grow/greek-word -logos-meaning/#meaning.

43. Online Etymology Dictionary, s.v. "sermon," accessed April 11, 2024, www.etymonline.com/word/sermon.

44. Bob Henry, "In the Beginning Was the Conversation!" Indianapolis First Friends, January 23, 2022, www.indyfriends .org/messages/2022/1/13/1-23-22-in-the-beginning-was-the -conversation#:~:text=In%20the%20beginning%20was%20 the%20Conversation%2C%20and%20the%20Conversation%20 was,the%20light%20of%20all%20mankind.

45. C. A. L. Jarrott, "Erasmus' 'In Principio Erat Sermo': A Controversial Translation," *Studies in Philology*, vol. 61 (January 1964), 35–40, www.jstor.org/stable/4173446.

46. John 14:20.

47. John 15:9.

48. Ephesians 3:18–19.

49. John 17:3.

50. Psalms 27:8; 136:12.

51. Exodus 3:6.

52. Galatians 3:19.

53. Romans 6:6.

54. *The Conversations and Letters of Brother Lawrence concerning the Presence of God* (London: J. Hatchard, 1824), 20.

55. This quote is often attributed to Chinese philosopher Laozi. Quoted in Elijah John, *The Mystical Path of Christian Theosis: Practical Exercises for Experiencing Christian Purification, Illumination, and Glorification* (Reno, NV: Monastic Press, 2020), 53.

56. Mark 12:30.

57. Matthew 7:7.

58. Matthew 18:21–22.

59. 1 John 4:19.

60. Exodus 20:18 NKJV.

61. John 15:9.

62. John 14:6 NKJV.

63. Matthew 24:12 NLT.

64. Revelation 3:20.

65. Luke 19:10 NKJV.

66. Psalm 139.

67. John 16:8.

68. John 16:13–15.

69. John 10:10; Revelation 12:12.

70. Psalm 42:5.

71. Isaiah 53:3.

72. James 1:2; Romans 5:3 ESV; 1 Peter 3:14.

73. Christopher West, *Fill These Hearts: God, Sex, and the Universal Longing* (New York: Image, 2013), 35.

74. Psalm 63:1 paraphrase.

75. Isaiah 61:3 paraphrase.

76. Genesis 2:25.

77. Ephesians 1:4–5.

78. 1 Peter 1:20.

79. Genesis 3:7 NLT.

80. Genesis 3:8.

81. Psalm 139:2–4.

82. Merriam-Webster's Online Dictionary, s.v. "shame," accessed May 16, 2024, www.merriam-webster.com/dictionary/shame #:~:text=Synonyms%20of%20shame-,1,the%20susceptibility%20 to%20such%20emotion.

83. Online Etymology Dictionary, s.v. "shame," accessed April 14, 2024, www.etymonline.com/word/shame.

84. *Baker's Evangelical Dictionary of Biblical Theology*, s.v. "repentance," ed. Walter E. Elwell (Grand Rapids, MI: Baker Books, 1996); Bible Study Tools, "Repentance," accessed April 15, 2024, www.biblestudytools.com/dictionary/repentance/.

85. Joshua Elzner, *Responding to the Thirst of God: 40 Days to the Heart of Love* (self-published, 2022), 86.

86. 2 Corinthians 3:18.

87. Genesis 3:9.

88. Luke 6:29.

89. Romans 8:26.

90. John 20:11–16.

91. John 19:41.

92. Isaac Ambrose, *Looking unto Jesus: A View of the Everlasting Gospel; or, The Soul's Eyeing of Jesus, as Carrying on the Great Work of Man's Salvation, from First to Last* (Philadelphia: J. B. Lippincott, 1856), 332.

93. John 15:5.

94. John 15:1–2.

95. Charles Spurgeon, "Supposing Him to Be the Gardener," sermon, Metropolitan Tabernacle Pulpit, vol. 29, December 31, 1882, Spurgeon Center, accessed April 15, 2024, www.spurgeon .org/resource-library/sermons/supposing-him-to-be-the -gardner/#flipbook/.

96. 1 John 4:19 NASB.

97. Ephesians 1:14.

98. 1 John 3:2 ESV.

99. Psalm 34:8.

Bible Credits